AF854393

Mobile App Hacking and Defense Strategies

How Cybercriminals Attack Mobile Apps and How to Defend Yourself Against Modern Mobile Threats

By Joe Correa

Published by Live Stronger Faster

Copyright © 2026 by Joe Correa

All rights reserved.

No part of this publication may be reproduced, distributed, or transmitted in any form or by any means—electronic, mechanical, photocopying, recording, or otherwise—without the prior written permission of the publisher, except in the case of brief quotations embodied in critical reviews and certain other noncommercial uses permitted by copyright law.

This book is for educational and informational purposes only. The author and publisher are not engaged in rendering legal, financial, or other professional advice. Readers should consult a qualified professional before making any financial decisions.

First Edition

Table of Contents

Introduction

The smartphone has become one of the most powerful tools ever created. It serves as a communication device, personal assistant, digital wallet, entertainment center, navigation system, health tracker, and gateway to nearly every aspect of modern life. Millions of people rely on mobile applications every day to manage finances, communicate with loved ones, conduct business, store sensitive documents, share photos, and access online services. While these technologies have created extraordinary convenience, they have also created an enormous opportunity for cybercriminals. Mobile applications have become some of the most attractive targets in the digital world because they often contain valuable personal information, financial data, login credentials, and access to numerous online accounts.

Most smartphone users assume that downloading an app from an official app store automatically guarantees safety. While official stores provide important security controls, no platform is completely immune to threats. Cybercriminals continuously search for new ways to exploit weaknesses in mobile applications, manipulate users, steal data, install malware, and gain unauthorized access to devices. Every year, attackers develop increasingly sophisticated techniques designed specifically for mobile platforms. As smartphones become more powerful and interconnected, the rewards for successful attacks continue to grow.

The reality is that most successful mobile attacks do not occur because hackers possess extraordinary technical abilities. Instead, many attacks succeed because users are unaware of the risks they face. Mobile security is not solely about technology. It is also about understanding how cybercriminals think, how they identify targets, how they exploit vulnerabilities, and how they manipulate human behavior. By understanding the methods used by attackers, individuals can dramatically reduce their risk of becoming victims.

This book was created to provide a practical understanding of mobile app hacking and defense strategies. Its purpose is not to teach readers how to commit cybercrime or exploit software illegally. Instead, it aims to help readers understand how attacks occur so they can better defend themselves, their families, and their organizations. Knowledge is one of the most effective cybersecurity tools available. The more you understand about the techniques attackers use, the better equipped you will be to recognize warning signs and implement effective protection measures.

Many people imagine hackers as mysterious individuals sitting in dark rooms surrounded by computer screens. While such stereotypes persist in movies and popular culture, the reality is far more complex. Modern cybercriminals range from organized criminal groups and nation-state actors to opportunistic scammers and automated attack systems. Some attackers target individuals, while others target businesses, governments, healthcare providers, financial institutions, or educational organizations. Mobile applications often serve as entry points into larger systems, making them valuable targets for attackers seeking access to broader networks and resources.

One reason mobile applications attract attackers is the sheer volume of sensitive information they contain. Consider how many apps on a typical smartphone store personal information. Banking apps provide access to financial accounts. Email applications contain sensitive communications. Social media platforms store personal details, photos, locations, and social connections. Shopping applications maintain payment information. Healthcare applications may contain medical records and health data. Productivity applications often store business documents and confidential information. For cybercriminals, compromising a single device can provide access to a treasure trove of valuable data.

The growth of mobile commerce has also increased security risks. Millions of transactions occur daily through mobile payment platforms, banking applications, digital wallets, and online marketplaces. As financial activity shifts toward smartphones, attackers increasingly focus on methods designed to intercept payments, steal credentials, capture authentication codes, and manipulate financial transactions. Criminals recognize that financial information can often be converted directly into profit, making mobile financial applications particularly attractive targets.

Beyond financial gain, cybercriminals may pursue other objectives. Some attackers seek personal information for identity theft. Others collect data for blackmail, surveillance, corporate espionage, or political purposes. In some cases, attackers use compromised devices to launch additional attacks against other victims. Smartphones connected to larger networks can become valuable components in criminal operations, allowing attackers to expand their reach while concealing their activities.

One of the most important concepts readers will learn throughout this book is that cybersecurity is an ongoing process rather than a single action. There is no single application, setting, or tool capable of providing complete protection against every threat. Effective security requires multiple layers of defense working together. This concept, often referred to as defense in depth, involves combining technical safeguards, user awareness, strong authentication practices, secure software usage, and continuous monitoring. Even if one layer fails, other protective measures can help prevent a successful attack.

A significant challenge in mobile cybersecurity is the constantly evolving nature of threats. Attack methods that were effective five years ago may no longer work today. Likewise, new technologies often create new opportunities for attackers. As mobile operating systems evolve and app developers introduce innovative features, cybercriminals continuously adapt their strategies. Security professionals must therefore remain vigilant, constantly learning about emerging threats and developing new defensive techniques.

Another important topic explored throughout this book is the role of software vulnerabilities. Every application is created by humans, and human-created systems inevitably contain flaws. Some vulnerabilities result from programming mistakes, while others emerge from design weaknesses or configuration errors. Attackers actively search for these weaknesses because vulnerabilities can provide pathways into systems that would otherwise remain secure. Understanding how vulnerabilities arise and how developers address them helps users appreciate the importance of software updates and secure development practices.

The human factor remains one of the most exploited elements in cybersecurity. Even the most secure applications can become vulnerable when users are deceived into revealing passwords, approving malicious permissions, or downloading harmful software. Social engineering attacks continue to be among the most successful methods used by cybercriminals because they target human psychology rather than technical systems. Attackers frequently exploit trust, fear, urgency, curiosity, and emotion to manipulate victims into making dangerous decisions. Developing awareness of these tactics is a critical component of mobile security.

Throughout this book, readers will encounter discussions about malware specifically designed for mobile environments. Mobile malware comes in many forms, including spyware, banking trojans, ransomware, adware, credential stealers, remote access tools, and surveillance software. Some malware operates openly, while other forms remain hidden for extended periods. Attackers often design malicious software to blend seamlessly into normal device activity, making detection difficult without proper security knowledge and tools.

Readers will also learn about common attack vectors used against mobile applications. These include insecure data storage, weak authentication systems, improper encryption, insecure communication channels, malicious code injection, application tampering, reverse engineering, phishing attacks, and third-party library vulnerabilities. Understanding these attack methods allows users to evaluate risks more effectively and adopt safer digital habits.

While understanding threats is important, this book places equal emphasis on defense strategies. Every chapter is designed to help readers implement practical protective measures that reduce exposure to risk. Topics include secure app installation practices, permission management, software updates, encryption, multifactor authentication, network security, malware prevention, privacy protection, and incident response. Readers will learn not only how attacks occur but also how to build a stronger personal security posture.

One of the most empowering aspects of cybersecurity education is the realization that many threats can be mitigated through relatively simple actions. Keeping software updated, enabling multifactor authentication, avoiding suspicious links, verifying application sources, monitoring permissions, and practicing secure password management can dramatically improve security. While no system can be made completely invulnerable, informed users can significantly reduce the likelihood of becoming victims.

As mobile devices continue to integrate with smart homes, wearable technology, vehicles, healthcare systems, and business environments, mobile security will become increasingly important. Smartphones are no longer isolated devices. They are central hubs connected to countless digital services and physical systems. A compromise affecting one mobile device can potentially impact many other connected technologies. Understanding how to protect mobile applications therefore contributes to broader digital safety and resilience.

The goal of this book is to transform readers from passive technology users into informed digital defenders. By understanding the techniques used by attackers and learning effective defense strategies, readers can make smarter decisions about the applications they install, the information they share, and the security measures they implement. Cybersecurity is not reserved for technical experts. Every smartphone user can benefit from learning the principles of mobile app security and applying them in everyday life.

As you begin this journey into mobile app hacking and defense strategies, remember that cybersecurity is ultimately about awareness, preparation, and continuous learning. The threats facing mobile users will continue to evolve, but so will the tools and techniques available to defend against them. By developing a strong understanding of both offensive and defensive perspectives, you will be better prepared to protect your devices, your information, your finances, and your digital future. This knowledge will serve as a valuable foundation as we explore the modern landscape of mobile application security and the practical strategies required to stay safe in an increasingly connected world.

Chapter 1

Understanding the Mobile App Threat Landscape

The first step toward protecting yourself from mobile app attacks is understanding the threat landscape that exists today. Many smartphone users believe cyberattacks primarily target large corporations, government agencies, or wealthy individuals. In reality, everyday smartphone users are among the most common targets. Mobile devices contain valuable information that cybercriminals can exploit for financial gain, identity theft, fraud, surveillance, and other malicious purposes. Understanding the risks that exist in the mobile ecosystem helps users make better security decisions and recognize potential threats before they become victims.

Modern smartphones hold a tremendous amount of sensitive information. They contain personal photographs, emails, text messages, banking information, login credentials, contact lists, health data, location history, and access to social media accounts. Many people use their phones to manage nearly every aspect of their daily lives. Because smartphones serve as central hubs for personal and professional activities, they represent attractive targets for cybercriminals seeking valuable information. A single compromised device can provide attackers with access to numerous accounts and services.

One of the primary reasons mobile devices attract attackers is the growing popularity of mobile applications. Mobile apps provide convenience by allowing users to perform tasks quickly from anywhere. However, every application installed on a device introduces a potential security risk. Applications are software programs created by developers, and all software contains the possibility of vulnerabilities. Some vulnerabilities arise from coding mistakes, while others result from poor security design, inadequate testing, or insecure third-party components. Attackers continuously search for these weaknesses because they can serve as entry points into devices and accounts.

The mobile threat landscape includes a wide variety of attack methods. Malware remains one of the most common threats facing smartphone users. Malware is a broad term that refers to malicious software designed to harm systems, steal information, spy on users, or generate profits for attackers. Mobile malware can be disguised as legitimate applications, hidden inside modified versions of popular software, or delivered through phishing campaigns. Once installed, malware may operate silently in the background while collecting information or performing unauthorized actions.

Spyware represents one particularly dangerous category of mobile malware. Spyware is designed to monitor user activities without consent. It may collect text messages, call logs, emails, location information, browsing history, and even microphone or camera recordings. Some spyware applications are highly sophisticated and difficult to detect. In certain cases, victims may remain unaware that their devices have been compromised for months or even years. Understanding how spyware operates helps users identify suspicious behaviors and implement stronger security practices.

Another common threat involves phishing attacks. Phishing occurs when attackers attempt to trick users into revealing sensitive information. Mobile phishing attacks often arrive through email messages, text messages, social media platforms, or messaging applications. Attackers frequently impersonate trusted organizations such as banks, online retailers, government agencies, or popular technology companies. Their goal is to create a sense of urgency that encourages victims to click malicious links, download harmful files, or provide confidential information. Because smartphones have smaller screens than computers, users may find it more difficult to recognize fraudulent websites and warning signs.

Financially motivated cybercriminals increasingly target mobile banking and payment applications. Banking trojans are a specialized type of malware designed to steal financial information. These malicious programs may capture login credentials, intercept authentication codes, record keystrokes, or display fake login screens that mimic legitimate banking apps. Once attackers obtain account access, they may initiate unauthorized transactions or sell stolen information to other criminals. Financial fraud remains one of the primary motivations behind many mobile attacks.

Social engineering plays a major role in mobile security incidents. Rather than directly attacking software, social engineering targets human psychology. Attackers manipulate emotions such as fear, curiosity, trust, excitement, or urgency to influence behavior. For example, a user may receive a message claiming that a package delivery failed or that a financial account requires immediate verification. Acting without careful examination, the user may unknowingly provide information that helps attackers achieve their goals. Developing awareness of social engineering tactics is one of the most effective defenses against many forms of cybercrime.

Mobile application permissions represent another important aspect of the threat landscape. Applications often request access to device features such as cameras, microphones, contacts, location services, and storage. While many permissions are necessary for legitimate functionality, excessive or unnecessary permissions can create privacy and security risks. Some applications collect significantly more information than they require to operate. Users who grant permissions without understanding their purpose may unintentionally expose sensitive information. Learning to evaluate permission requests is an essential mobile security skill.

Public Wi-Fi networks introduce additional risks. Many users connect their smartphones to free Wi-Fi networks in airports, hotels, restaurants, coffee shops, and public venues. While convenient, public networks may expose users to various security threats. Attackers sometimes create fake Wi-Fi hotspots designed to intercept traffic or collect login credentials. In other cases, unsecured networks allow attackers to monitor communications between devices and online services. Understanding how network-based attacks occur helps users make safer decisions when connecting to unfamiliar networks.

Another significant concern involves insecure application development practices. Developers sometimes prioritize convenience, speed, or functionality over security. As a result, applications may store sensitive information improperly, use weak encryption, transmit data insecurely, or fail to validate user inputs adequately. These weaknesses create opportunities for attackers to exploit vulnerabilities and gain unauthorized access. Although users cannot directly control how applications are developed, understanding these risks helps them choose software more carefully and remain alert to potential issues.

Third-party software libraries also contribute to the complexity of the mobile threat landscape. Modern applications frequently incorporate external code components developed by other organizations. These libraries provide useful features and reduce development time, but they may introduce security vulnerabilities. If attackers discover weaknesses in commonly used libraries, they can potentially affect thousands of applications simultaneously. This interconnected environment means that vulnerabilities in one component can have widespread consequences across the mobile ecosystem.

The rise of artificial intelligence has begun influencing both cybersecurity defenses and cyberattacks. Attackers increasingly use automated tools to identify targets, create convincing phishing messages, and analyze stolen data. At the same time, security professionals use artificial intelligence to detect threats, identify suspicious activities, and improve defensive capabilities. As technology evolves, both attackers and defenders continue adapting their strategies, creating an ongoing cycle of innovation and countermeasures.

Supply chain attacks represent another emerging threat. Rather than attacking users directly, cybercriminals compromise software providers, developers, or distribution channels. By infiltrating trusted systems, attackers can distribute malicious updates or modified applications to large numbers of users. Supply chain attacks are particularly dangerous because victims often trust software from reputable sources. Understanding this threat highlights the importance of maintaining multiple layers of defense rather than relying solely on trust.

Identity theft remains one of the most damaging consequences of mobile security breaches. Stolen personal information may be used to open financial accounts, commit fraud, access services, or impersonate victims online. Recovering from identity theft can require significant time, effort, and financial resources. Protecting personal information is therefore not only a privacy concern but also an important financial and legal consideration.

The threat landscape will continue evolving as mobile technology advances. New applications, devices, communication methods, and services will create both opportunities and risks. Security is not a destination but an ongoing process of learning, adaptation, and awareness. Individuals who understand the nature of mobile threats are better positioned to recognize warning signs, evaluate risks, and make informed decisions that reduce their exposure to cybercrime.

Developing a security mindset is one of the most valuable lessons readers can take from this chapter. A security mindset involves questioning unexpected requests, verifying information before taking action, maintaining awareness of potential risks, and understanding that convenience sometimes comes with security tradeoffs. Users who approach technology thoughtfully are less likely to become victims of common attacks. Knowledge, vigilance, and responsible digital habits form the foundation of effective mobile security.

As we move through the remainder of this book, you will learn how specific attacks work, how attackers exploit vulnerabilities, and how practical defense strategies can protect your devices and personal information. Understanding the threat landscape provides the foundation upon which all other mobile security skills are built. By recognizing the risks that exist, you become better equipped to defend yourself in an increasingly connected and complex digital world.

David began studying cybersecurity

David considered himself reasonably tech-savvy. At thirty-eight years old, he managed a successful consulting business, communicated with clients through mobile applications, handled banking transactions from his smartphone, and maintained active social media accounts. Like many people, he relied on his phone throughout the day. It served as his calendar, communication device, navigation system, entertainment center, and financial management tool. He believed he understood technology well enough to avoid most online dangers.

One Monday morning, David received a text message claiming to be from a package delivery company. The message stated that a shipment could not be delivered due to an address verification issue. Since David had recently ordered several products online, the message seemed legitimate. Without giving it much thought, he tapped the link and arrived at a professional-looking website. The page requested basic information to confirm delivery details. David entered his name, address, and phone number before closing the page and continuing with his day.

Several days later, unusual activity began appearing on his accounts. First, he noticed login alerts from unfamiliar locations. Then he received emails indicating password reset requests for several services. Soon after, unauthorized purchases appeared on one of his credit cards. Confused and concerned, David contacted his bank and began investigating the situation. He struggled to understand how attackers had gained access to his information.

As he worked with security specialists, David learned that the delivery message had been part of a sophisticated phishing campaign. The website he visited had collected personal information that attackers used to build a profile of him. Using information gathered from multiple sources, the criminals launched additional attacks targeting his online accounts. The attackers combined social engineering with publicly available information to increase their chances of success.

Determined to prevent future incidents, David began studying cybersecurity. He quickly discovered that mobile threats were far more complex than he had realized. He learned about phishing attacks, malware, spyware, credential theft, and social engineering. The more he learned, the more he recognized how many risks existed within the digital environment he used every day. His experience demonstrated that attackers often succeed not because victims are careless, but because threats are designed to appear trustworthy and convincing.

Several months later, David attended a cybersecurity workshop organized by a local technology association. During the event, participants reviewed real-world attack scenarios. One presentation focused on mobile applications requesting excessive permissions. The instructor demonstrated how seemingly harmless applications could collect extensive personal information when granted unnecessary access. David remembered routinely approving permission requests without reading them carefully. He began reevaluating the applications installed on his phone and discovered several apps that had access to data they did not truly need.

As David continued improving his security habits, he started helping friends and family understand mobile risks. His younger sister, Emily, frequently downloaded games and entertainment applications without researching developers or reviewing permissions. David explained how malicious applications sometimes disguise themselves as legitimate software. He showed her how to evaluate app reviews, examine developer information, and limit unnecessary permissions. Emily was surprised to learn how much information certain apps attempted to collect.

One evening, David's father received a phone call from someone claiming to represent his bank's fraud department. The caller stated that suspicious activity had been detected and requested account verification information. Remembering the lessons David had shared, his father refused to provide information and contacted the bank directly using the number listed on his card. The bank confirmed that no fraud representative had called. The attempted scam had failed because awareness and verification practices prevented the attacker from succeeding.

Over time, David developed what cybersecurity professionals call a security mindset. Instead of reacting immediately to unexpected messages, he paused to evaluate situations carefully. He verified requests through trusted channels, maintained strong authentication practices, reviewed application permissions regularly, and kept his devices updated. These habits became second nature. Rather than viewing security as a burden, he began seeing it as an important part of responsible technology use.

A year after the phishing incident, David reflected on how much his perspective had changed. He realized that cybersecurity was not about living in fear of technology. Instead, it was about understanding risks and making informed decisions. His smartphone remained an incredibly useful tool, but he now recognized that convenience and security must work together. The knowledge he gained allowed him to enjoy technology while minimizing unnecessary risks.

David's journey illustrates an important lesson for every smartphone user. Mobile threats are real, but users are not powerless. Understanding how cybercriminals operate, recognizing common attack techniques, and developing good security habits can dramatically reduce risk. While no system can guarantee complete protection, informed users are far less likely to become easy targets.

As technology continues evolving, new threats will inevitably emerge. However, the fundamental principles David learned remain timeless. Awareness, skepticism, verification, and continuous learning form the foundation of effective cybersecurity. Individuals who cultivate these habits build resilience against both current and future threats.

The story of David serves as a reminder that cybersecurity is not reserved for experts, programmers, or security professionals. Every smartphone user benefits from understanding the threat landscape. Every user can learn to recognize warning signs. Every user can take practical steps to strengthen security. In an increasingly connected world, knowledge remains one of the most powerful defenses available.

By understanding the mobile app threat landscape, David transformed from a potential victim into an informed defender. The same transformation is possible for anyone willing to learn, remain vigilant, and apply the principles of mobile security in everyday life. The lessons introduced in this chapter will provide the foundation for the more advanced concepts and defense strategies explored throughout the rest of this book.

Chapter 2

How Cybercriminals Attack Mobile Applications

Understanding how cybercriminals attack mobile applications is one of the most important steps toward building effective defenses. Many smartphone users believe attacks occur randomly or require extraordinary technical skill, but most successful mobile attacks follow predictable patterns. Cybercriminals carefully study their targets, identify weaknesses, and exploit vulnerabilities that provide the greatest chance of success. By understanding how these attacks work, users can recognize warning signs and reduce the likelihood of becoming victims.

Mobile applications are attractive targets because they often serve as gateways to valuable information and services. Banking apps provide access to financial accounts. Email applications contain sensitive communications. Social media platforms reveal personal information and relationships. Business applications may provide access to corporate systems and confidential documents. Rather than attacking every user directly, cybercriminals frequently focus on compromising mobile applications because doing so can provide access to large amounts of valuable data.

One of the most common attack methods involves exploiting software vulnerabilities. A vulnerability is a weakness in an application's design, code, or configuration that can be abused by attackers. Vulnerabilities may arise from programming errors, inadequate security testing, or improper handling of sensitive data. Even experienced developers occasionally make mistakes, and cybercriminals constantly search for flaws that can be turned into opportunities for unauthorized access.

Attackers often use automated scanning tools to identify vulnerable applications. These tools analyze software behavior, network communications, and application code for weaknesses. Once a vulnerability is discovered, attackers may attempt to exploit it before developers release a patch. This race between attackers and defenders is a constant aspect of cybersecurity. The longer a vulnerability remains unpatched, the greater the risk to users.

Reverse engineering is another common technique used by cybercriminals. Reverse engineering involves analyzing an application's code and behavior to understand how it works internally. Attackers use specialized tools to examine application files, identify hidden functions, locate sensitive information, and uncover weaknesses. While reverse engineering has legitimate uses in software testing and security research, it can also be used for malicious purposes.

Attackers may reverse engineer applications to discover authentication mechanisms, encryption keys, or vulnerabilities that can be exploited.

Code injection attacks represent another major threat. In a code injection attack, an attacker inserts malicious commands into an application or system. If the application fails to validate inputs properly, the injected code may execute with the application's privileges. This can lead to unauthorized access, data theft, or system compromise. Input validation is therefore one of the most important security practices in application development.

Attackers frequently target authentication systems because login credentials provide direct access to user accounts. Credential theft can occur through phishing attacks, malware, fake login screens, or intercepted communications. Once attackers obtain usernames and passwords, they can access accounts, steal information, and impersonate users. Weak passwords, password reuse, and lack of multifactor authentication significantly increase the likelihood of successful credential-based attacks.

Session hijacking is another technique used to compromise user accounts. After a user successfully authenticates, applications typically create a session that allows continued access without repeatedly entering credentials. If attackers obtain session tokens or authentication cookies, they may be able to impersonate users without needing passwords. Session hijacking can occur through insecure network communications, malware infections, or vulnerabilities in application design.

Cybercriminals also exploit insecure data storage practices. Many applications store information locally on devices to improve performance and user convenience. However, if sensitive data such as passwords, authentication tokens, personal information, or financial records are stored improperly, attackers who gain access to the device may retrieve this information. Secure storage practices are essential for protecting sensitive data from unauthorized access.

Network-based attacks remain common in mobile environments. Smartphones frequently connect to public Wi-Fi networks, cellular networks, and other communication channels. Attackers may attempt to intercept data transmitted between applications and servers. Man-in-the-middle attacks occur when attackers position themselves between communicating parties and secretly monitor or modify data exchanges. Without proper encryption, sensitive information may be exposed during transmission.

Application tampering represents another significant threat. Attackers sometimes modify legitimate applications to include malicious functionality. These modified applications may appear identical to the original versions while secretly collecting information, displaying advertisements, or installing malware. Users who download software from unofficial sources face increased risk because modified applications are commonly distributed through unauthorized channels.

Malware developers often use trojanized applications to infect devices. A trojanized app appears legitimate but contains hidden malicious code. Users willingly install the application because they believe it provides useful functionality. Once installed, the malware begins executing its malicious activities. Trojans may steal credentials, spy on users, intercept communications, or grant remote access to attackers.

Privilege escalation attacks occur when attackers gain higher levels of access than intended. Mobile operating systems use permission systems to restrict what applications can do. However, vulnerabilities sometimes allow attackers to bypass these restrictions and obtain elevated privileges. Once elevated access is achieved, attackers can access protected resources, modify system settings, or compromise other applications.

Attackers increasingly target third-party software libraries used by mobile applications. Developers frequently incorporate external libraries to provide functionality such as analytics, advertising, payment processing, and communication services. While these libraries offer convenience, vulnerabilities within them can affect many applications simultaneously. A single vulnerable component may create risks across thousands of applications.

Social engineering remains one of the most effective attack methods because it targets human behavior rather than technology. Attackers understand that users often trust familiar brands, respond to urgent requests, and seek convenience. By creating convincing messages and scenarios, cybercriminals can persuade victims to install malicious software, reveal credentials, or grant excessive permissions. Technical defenses alone cannot fully prevent social engineering attacks, making user awareness critical.

Phishing applications represent a growing threat. Attackers create fake applications designed to mimic legitimate services. These counterfeit apps may closely resemble banking apps, social media platforms, shopping services, or productivity tools. Users who install and interact with these applications may unknowingly provide credentials and personal information directly to attackers. Careful verification of application sources helps reduce this risk.

Mobile ransomware has also emerged as a serious concern. Ransomware encrypts files or restricts access to devices until victims pay a ransom. Although mobile ransomware is less common than desktop ransomware, it continues evolving. Some variants lock screens, encrypt data, or threaten to release sensitive information unless payment is made. Maintaining backups and avoiding suspicious downloads are important defenses against ransomware.

Cybercriminals often combine multiple attack techniques to increase effectiveness. A phishing message may deliver malware. Malware may steal credentials. Stolen credentials may enable account compromise. Account compromise may lead to financial fraud or identity theft. Understanding how attacks chain together helps users appreciate the importance of layered security measures.

The cybersecurity industry frequently refers to the attack lifecycle. Attackers typically begin with reconnaissance, gathering information about targets and identifying vulnerabilities. Next comes initial access, where attackers gain entry through phishing, malware, or exploited weaknesses. Once access is established, attackers may expand privileges, move through systems, collect information, and achieve their objectives. Recognizing this lifecycle helps defenders identify opportunities to interrupt attacks before significant damage occurs.

Mobile security depends on understanding both attacker techniques and defensive strategies. Every attack method described in this chapter exploits a specific weakness. Some weaknesses involve software vulnerabilities. Others involve poor security practices or human error. By understanding how cybercriminals operate, users become better equipped to recognize risks and implement effective safeguards.

The most important lesson is that cybercriminals are constantly adapting. New technologies create new opportunities for attack, while security improvements force attackers to develop more sophisticated methods. Effective defense therefore requires continuous learning, awareness, and adaptation. The better you understand attacker behavior, the more effectively you can protect yourself against evolving threats.

As we continue through this book, you will learn specific defensive techniques designed to counter the attacks discussed in this chapter. Understanding how attacks occur provides a strong foundation for developing practical security habits that protect both your devices and your personal information.

The experience shocked Michael

Michael enjoyed technology and considered himself an early adopter. Whenever a new application became popular, he was usually among the first of his friends to try it. His smartphone contained dozens of apps for productivity, entertainment, social networking, shopping, and banking. He appreciated the convenience these applications provided and rarely worried about security. Like many users, he assumed that most threats happened to other people.

One afternoon, Michael noticed an advertisement promoting a premium version of a popular photo-editing application. The advertisement claimed the modified version included advanced features normally available only through a paid subscription. Curious and interested in saving money, he downloaded the application from a website rather than the official app store. The installation process appeared normal, and the application worked exactly as advertised.

Over the following weeks, however, unusual events began occurring. Michael occasionally noticed his phone becoming warm even when he was not actively using it. Battery life declined significantly. Some applications appeared to consume more data than expected. Although these symptoms seemed minor, they were early warning signs that something was wrong.

Unknown to Michael, the application he installed had been modified by cybercriminals. The attackers had reverse engineered the original software, inserted malicious code, and redistributed the application through unofficial channels. While the app provided the promised photo-editing features, it also secretly collected information from his device and transmitted data to remote servers controlled by attackers.

The malware monitored login credentials entered into various applications. It recorded information about installed software, device identifiers, and browsing activity. The attackers patiently collected information, waiting for opportunities to exploit valuable accounts. Because the malicious activity operated quietly in the background, Michael remained unaware of the compromise.

Several weeks later, Michael received an email notification from his bank indicating a login attempt from another state. Concerned, he changed his password immediately. Unfortunately, the malware captured the new password as well. The attackers now possessed both account credentials and information about his device. They used this information to bypass certain security checks and gain access to his financial accounts.

Fortunately, the bank's fraud detection systems identified suspicious transactions and temporarily froze the account. Michael contacted customer support and began investigating what had happened. During the investigation, cybersecurity specialists examined his device and identified the malicious application. They explained how attackers frequently modify legitimate apps and distribute them outside official stores.

The experience shocked Michael. He had always assumed malware required obvious signs such as pop-up advertisements, device crashes, or visible damage. Instead, he learned that modern mobile malware often operates quietly and strategically. The attackers were not interested in causing immediate disruption. Their goal was to collect information gradually and maximize financial gain.

Determined to learn more, Michael enrolled in a cybersecurity awareness course offered through his employer. The course covered topics such as phishing, malware, application security, and social engineering. During one exercise, participants analyzed simulated attacks and identified the techniques used by cybercriminals. Michael began recognizing patterns he had previously overlooked.

One lesson focused on the attack lifecycle. Participants learned how attackers gather information, gain access, escalate privileges, and achieve objectives. Michael realized his own experience had followed this exact pattern. The attackers first distributed a trojanized application, then established access to his device, collected information, and eventually targeted financial accounts. Understanding the sequence helped him appreciate how seemingly small decisions can contribute to larger security incidents.

Over time, Michael adopted stronger security practices. He downloaded applications exclusively from trusted sources. He reviewed permissions carefully before installation. He enabled multifactor authentication on important accounts and monitored account activity regularly. He also learned how to recognize warning signs such as unusual battery usage, unexpected permissions, and suspicious network activity.

Several months later, Michael's coworker Sarah mentioned finding a website that offered free premium versions of popular applications. Remembering his own experience, Michael explained the risks associated with unofficial downloads. He described how attackers modify applications and use them to distribute malware. Sarah decided against installing the software and instead obtained the application through legitimate channels.

As Michael shared his experiences with others, he realized many people underestimated mobile security risks. Friends often assumed smartphones were automatically secure because of modern operating systems and app stores. While these protections are valuable, Michael understood that attackers continuously search for ways around them. Security requires both technological safeguards and informed user behavior.

A year after the incident, Michael looked back on the experience as a valuable lesson. Although the attack had caused stress and inconvenience, it motivated him to become more knowledgeable about cybersecurity. He no longer viewed security as something handled entirely by software developers or technology companies. Instead, he recognized that every user plays an important role in protecting their own information.

Michael's story demonstrates how cybercriminals exploit both technical vulnerabilities and human behavior. The attackers succeeded not because Michael lacked intelligence, but because they understood how to make their malicious application appear attractive and trustworthy. Their strategy relied on convenience, curiosity, and the desire to access premium features without cost.

The lesson is clear. Understanding how cybercriminals attack mobile applications helps users recognize risks before problems occur. Attackers rely on predictable techniques, and informed users can often identify warning signs early. By learning how attacks work, individuals gain the knowledge necessary to make safer decisions and strengthen their defenses.

As mobile technology continues evolving, cybercriminals will continue adapting their methods. However, the fundamental principles remain the same. Awareness, verification, caution, and continuous learning are among the strongest defenses available. By understanding attacker strategies and applying secure practices consistently, users can significantly reduce their risk of becoming victims and enjoy the benefits of mobile technology with greater confidence and security.

Chapter 3

Malware, Spyware, and Trojan Attacks on Mobile Devices

Malware is one of the most significant threats facing mobile device users today. As smartphones have become central to personal, financial, and professional activities, cybercriminals have increasingly focused on developing malicious software specifically designed to target mobile platforms. Understanding how malware operates, how it spreads, and how it affects devices is essential for anyone seeking to protect their personal information and maintain a secure digital environment. In this chapter, we will explore the major categories of mobile malware, including spyware and trojans, while examining the tactics cybercriminals use to compromise devices and the defensive strategies that can reduce risk.

The term malware is short for "malicious software." Malware refers to any software intentionally created to perform harmful actions without the user's knowledge or consent. Unlike legitimate applications that provide useful functionality, malware is designed to benefit attackers. These benefits may include stealing information, generating revenue, spying on users, gaining unauthorized access, disrupting operations, or facilitating additional attacks. Mobile malware has evolved significantly over the years and now exists in many forms, each designed to achieve specific objectives.

One reason malware has become so widespread is the enormous value of information stored on smartphones. Mobile devices contain personal communications, financial records, authentication credentials, photos, videos, contacts, location histories, and access to numerous online services. For cybercriminals, a compromised smartphone can provide access to far more information than many traditional computers. This concentration of valuable data makes smartphones highly attractive targets.

Mobile malware often begins with a seemingly harmless action by the user. An individual may download an application from an unofficial source, click a malicious link, open a suspicious attachment, scan a fraudulent QR code, or approve permissions without fully understanding the consequences. Attackers frequently rely on deception rather than technical sophistication. Their goal is to persuade users to voluntarily install software that appears legitimate while secretly performing malicious activities.

Trojans are among the most common forms of mobile malware. A trojan is a malicious program disguised as a legitimate application. The name originates from the ancient story of the Trojan Horse, where attackers concealed their true intentions inside what appeared to be a harmless gift. Modern trojans operate similarly. Users willingly install the software because it appears useful, entertaining, or beneficial. Once installed, the hidden malicious code begins executing.

Mobile trojans may perform a wide variety of actions. Some collect login credentials and authentication information. Others monitor user activity, intercept communications, or download additional malware. Certain trojans focus on financial fraud by targeting banking applications and payment platforms. Others create backdoors that allow attackers to remotely control devices. The versatility of trojans makes them one of the most dangerous threats in the mobile ecosystem.

Spyware represents another highly concerning category of malware. Unlike many other forms of malicious software, spyware is specifically designed to monitor and collect information. Its primary objective is surveillance. Spyware may record text messages, emails, phone calls, browsing activity, location data, and application usage. Advanced spyware may activate cameras and microphones without user awareness, transforming a smartphone into a surveillance device.

Many victims never realize spyware has been installed on their devices. Modern spyware often operates silently in the background while avoiding actions that would attract attention. It may consume minimal resources, limit network activity, and hide its presence from security tools. This stealthy behavior allows attackers to collect information over extended periods. The longer spyware remains undetected, the greater the amount of information attackers can gather.

Banking malware is a specialized form of spyware and credential theft software. Cybercriminals recognize that financial information can often be converted directly into profit. Banking malware targets mobile banking applications, digital wallets, investment platforms, and payment services. Attackers may create fake login screens that appear identical to legitimate banking interfaces. When users enter credentials, the information is transmitted directly to attackers while the victim remains unaware.

Some banking malware intercepts two-factor authentication codes sent through text messages. Even users who employ strong passwords may become vulnerable if attackers can capture authentication tokens. As financial institutions continue improving security, cybercriminals continuously adapt their techniques to bypass new protections.

Understanding these evolving threats helps users appreciate the importance of layered security measures.

Ransomware has become increasingly common in the cybersecurity landscape. Mobile ransomware typically restricts access to a device or encrypts valuable data until a ransom payment is made. Some variants lock the screen and display threatening messages demanding payment. Others encrypt photos, documents, and files stored on the device. Attackers often pressure victims by imposing deadlines or threatening permanent data loss. Although paying a ransom may seem like a solution, security professionals generally discourage payment because it provides no guarantee of recovery and encourages future criminal activity.

Adware represents a less destructive but still problematic category of malware. Adware generates revenue by displaying excessive advertisements, redirecting users to marketing websites, or collecting data used for advertising purposes. While some ad-supported applications operate legitimately, malicious adware often engages in deceptive practices. Excessive advertising can reduce device performance, consume bandwidth, drain battery life, and expose users to additional security risks.

Cryptojacking malware has emerged alongside the growth of cryptocurrencies. Cryptojacking software secretly uses a device's processing power to mine digital currencies for attackers. Victims may notice reduced performance, overheating, excessive battery drain, or increased data usage. While cryptojacking may not directly steal information, it exploits device resources without permission and can shorten hardware lifespan through excessive resource consumption.

One important concept in mobile malware defense is understanding infection vectors. An infection vector refers to the method by which malware reaches a device. Common infection vectors include malicious applications, phishing emails, text message scams, compromised websites, social media links, infected advertisements, and unauthorized software downloads. Recognizing these delivery mechanisms helps users identify risky situations before malware gains access.

Attackers frequently use social engineering to distribute malware. Rather than exploiting technical weaknesses, they manipulate human behavior. Messages may claim that urgent action is required, that a reward is available, or that an account has been compromised. Fear, curiosity, urgency, and excitement are powerful emotional triggers that attackers exploit. Users who pause and verify information before acting are significantly less likely to fall victim to these tactics.

Mobile operating systems include numerous security controls designed to limit malware infections. Application sandboxing restricts what apps can access. Permission systems allow users to control sensitive features. Security updates address newly discovered vulnerabilities. Built-in security services scan applications for malicious behavior. However, these protections are most effective when users maintain good security habits and avoid unnecessary risks.

Software updates play a critical role in malware defense. Developers continuously identify and patch vulnerabilities that attackers might exploit. Delaying updates leaves devices exposed to known security weaknesses. Cybercriminals often target users who fail to install updates because publicly documented vulnerabilities provide attackers with ready-made attack opportunities. Regular updates significantly reduce the risk of compromise.

Another essential defense involves application source verification. Official app stores typically perform security reviews before distributing applications. While no review process is perfect, official stores generally provide significantly greater protection than unofficial sources. Applications obtained from unknown websites, file-sharing platforms, or unverified marketplaces present much higher risks. Users should carefully evaluate software sources before installation.

Permission management also serves as an important security practice. Applications should only receive access to resources necessary for their intended functionality. A flashlight app, for example, generally does not require access to contacts, microphones, or location services. Excessive permission requests may indicate privacy concerns or malicious intent. Reviewing permissions regularly helps users maintain greater control over personal information.

Behavioral monitoring can help identify potential malware infections. Symptoms such as unexpected battery drain, excessive data usage, unusual device heating, unauthorized account activity, unexplained advertisements, performance degradation, and unfamiliar applications may indicate compromise. While these symptoms do not always confirm malware, they warrant investigation. Early detection can significantly reduce the impact of an infection.

The most effective defense against malware combines technology, awareness, and good habits. Security software, operating system protections, strong authentication, careful downloading practices, regular updates, and user education all contribute to a stronger security posture. No single tool can eliminate all risks. Instead, successful security depends on multiple layers of protection working together.

As mobile threats continue evolving, users must remain informed and adaptable. Cybercriminals constantly develop new techniques, while defenders create new countermeasures. Understanding how malware, spyware, and trojans operate provides a strong foundation for protecting devices and personal information. Awareness transforms users from passive targets into active participants in their own security.

By recognizing the warning signs of infection, understanding attacker tactics, and implementing effective defensive practices, smartphone users can dramatically reduce their exposure to malware-related threats. The knowledge gained in this chapter will help readers build stronger defenses and make safer decisions in an increasingly connected digital world.

Jessica installed the app

Jessica owned a small graphic design business and depended heavily on her smartphone. She used it to communicate with clients, review project files, manage social media accounts, conduct online banking, and store business contacts. Her phone contained years of valuable information and served as an essential part of her daily operations. Like many busy professionals, she prioritized convenience and efficiency, rarely thinking about cybersecurity.

One afternoon, Jessica received a message through a social media platform from someone she believed was a former client. The message contained a link to what appeared to be a cloud storage folder containing design inspiration images. Curious and eager to see the content, she clicked the link. The website requested that she install a special mobile application to view the files. The application looked professional and included convincing screenshots and reviews.

Without much hesitation, Jessica installed the app. After installation, it requested several permissions, including access to storage, notifications, and contacts. The requests seemed reasonable for a file-sharing application, so she approved them. The app opened briefly, displayed an error message, and then closed. Assuming it was simply malfunctioning, Jessica deleted it and moved on with her day.

What Jessica did not realize was that the application had installed spyware before displaying the error message. Although the visible app was removed, hidden components remained active within the device. The spyware quietly began collecting information and transmitting it to remote servers operated by cybercriminals.

Over the following weeks, the spyware monitored Jessica's activities. It recorded login credentials, tracked application usage, captured contact information, and monitored financial transactions. The malware remained largely invisible, avoiding actions that might reveal its presence. Jessica occasionally noticed that her battery drained more quickly than usual, but she attributed the problem to normal device aging.

Several weeks later, unauthorized charges appeared on one of her business accounts. Shortly afterward, a client reported receiving suspicious messages that appeared to originate from Jessica's email address. Alarmed, she contacted her bank, changed passwords, and hired a cybersecurity consultant to investigate the situation.

The consultant performed a detailed examination of her device and discovered evidence of spyware infection. Jessica was shocked. She considered herself cautious and responsible, yet she had unknowingly installed malware through a simple act of curiosity. The consultant explained how attackers frequently disguise malicious software as useful applications. Their success depends on convincing users to lower their guard and trust what appears familiar.

Determined to prevent future incidents, Jessica began studying mobile security. She learned about trojans, spyware, ransomware, adware, and social engineering. The more she learned, the more she realized how sophisticated modern cybercriminals had become. Their attacks were not random. They were carefully planned operations designed to exploit both technology and human psychology.

As part of her recovery process, Jessica reviewed every application installed on her device. She removed unnecessary software, updated her operating system, enabled multifactor authentication, and began monitoring permissions more carefully. She also started verifying requests through independent channels before taking action. These habits gradually became part of her daily routine.

Several months later, Jessica attended a local business networking event where cybersecurity was discussed. During a panel discussion, many business owners admitted they had never considered mobile devices significant security risks. Jessica shared her experience and explained how a single malicious application had nearly compromised her business. Her story captured the audience's attention because it demonstrated how easily an ordinary user could become a target.

One attendee, Mark, later approached Jessica and described a similar situation. He had recently downloaded a modified version of a premium application from an unofficial website. Remembering her experience, Jessica encouraged him to scan his device and review his accounts. Security tools later discovered a trojan that had been collecting credentials from multiple applications. Because the infection was identified early, Mark avoided significant financial losses.

Over time, Jessica became an advocate for cybersecurity awareness among small business owners. She organized workshops, shared educational resources, and encouraged colleagues to treat smartphones with the same level of security attention given to computers and business networks. Her message was simple: smartphones contain enormous amounts of valuable information and deserve strong protection.

A year after the incident, Jessica reflected on the lessons she had learned. She no longer viewed cybersecurity as a technical specialty reserved for experts. Instead, she saw it as a practical life skill relevant to anyone who uses digital technology. Awareness, caution, and continuous learning had become essential components of her professional and personal routines.

Jessica's experience demonstrates how malware often succeeds through deception rather than technical complexity. The attackers did not force their way into her device. They persuaded her to install the software voluntarily by presenting it as something useful. This approach remains one of the most effective techniques used by cybercriminals because it exploits natural human tendencies such as curiosity and trust.

The story also highlights the importance of recognizing early warning signs. Unusual battery drain, unexpected account activity, performance issues, and suspicious messages can all indicate potential compromise. While these symptoms may have innocent explanations, investigating them promptly can prevent larger problems from developing.

Most importantly, Jessica learned that security is not achieved through a single action. It results from consistent habits, informed decisions, and a willingness to remain vigilant. Technology provides powerful security tools, but users must actively participate in protecting themselves. By understanding how malware, spyware, and trojans operate, individuals can make smarter choices and significantly reduce their risk of becoming victims.

As mobile devices continue playing larger roles in our lives, the lessons from Jessica's story become increasingly relevant.

Awareness remains one of the strongest defenses against cybercrime. Users who understand attacker tactics are better equipped to identify threats, avoid dangerous situations, and protect the valuable information stored within their devices. The knowledge gained in this chapter provides a foundation for stronger mobile security and prepares readers for the more advanced defense strategies explored throughout the remainder of this book.

Chapter 4

Phishing, Social Engineering, and Mobile App Scams

Among all the threats facing mobile device users today, phishing and social engineering remain some of the most successful and dangerous attack methods. Unlike malware attacks that often rely on technical vulnerabilities, phishing attacks target human psychology. Cybercriminals understand that even the most secure technology can be compromised if users are manipulated into providing information, clicking malicious links, or granting access voluntarily. Because smartphones are constantly connected and frequently used throughout the day, they provide attackers with numerous opportunities to exploit trust, curiosity, fear, urgency, and emotion.

Phishing is a form of cybercrime in which attackers attempt to trick individuals into revealing sensitive information. This information may include usernames, passwords, banking credentials, credit card numbers, authentication codes, personal identification details, or other valuable data. Phishing attacks often impersonate trusted organizations, such as banks, government agencies, technology companies, delivery services, social media platforms, or employers. The goal is to convince victims that the communication is legitimate and that immediate action is required.

The effectiveness of phishing attacks stems from the fact that attackers rarely need to defeat advanced security systems. Instead, they persuade users to provide access willingly. A successful phishing attack can bypass many technical safeguards because the victim unknowingly assists the attacker. This makes phishing one of the most cost-effective and profitable attack methods available to cybercriminals.

Mobile devices have introduced new challenges to phishing defense. Smartphone screens are smaller than computer monitors, making it more difficult to examine website addresses, security certificates, and other visual indicators of legitimacy. Users often process messages quickly while multitasking, traveling, or responding to notifications. These conditions create ideal opportunities for attackers who rely on impulsive decisions rather than careful analysis.

Email phishing remains one of the most common attack methods. Attackers send messages designed to appear as though they originate from trusted organizations. These messages may claim that an account has been suspended, a payment failed, a package is awaiting delivery, or suspicious activity has been detected. The message often contains a link directing the user to a fraudulent website. Once the victim enters credentials or personal information, the data is transmitted directly to attackers.

Mobile phishing has expanded beyond email into text messages, messaging apps, and social media platforms. Text message phishing, commonly known as smishing, has become particularly effective because many users trust text messages more than email. Attackers may impersonate banks, shipping companies, healthcare providers, or government agencies. Messages often contain urgent language designed to provoke immediate action before the victim has time to evaluate the situation carefully.

Voice phishing, sometimes referred to as vishing, involves phone calls rather than written messages. Attackers may use live operators or automated systems to impersonate customer service representatives, financial institutions, technical support personnel, or government officials. Victims are pressured into revealing sensitive information, authorizing transactions, or installing software. Because hearing a human voice often increases trust, voice phishing can be highly effective.

Social engineering encompasses a broader category of attacks that manipulate human behavior. While phishing is one form of social engineering, attackers use many other psychological techniques to achieve their goals. Social engineering exploits predictable aspects of human nature, including trust, curiosity, politeness, fear, greed, urgency, and the desire to help others. By understanding these emotional triggers, attackers create convincing scenarios that encourage victims to act against their own interests.

Urgency is one of the most frequently used social engineering tactics. Messages often claim that immediate action is required to avoid negative consequences. Examples include warnings about account suspension, unauthorized transactions, missed deliveries, expired subscriptions, or legal issues. When people feel rushed, they are more likely to make mistakes and less likely to verify information independently.

Fear is another powerful motivator. Attackers may claim that a device has been infected with malware, that personal information has been exposed, or that financial accounts are at risk. Fear encourages rapid decision-making and reduces critical thinking. Cybercriminals understand that anxious individuals often focus on solving the perceived problem rather than evaluating whether the warning itself is legitimate.

Curiosity can also be exploited effectively. Messages may reference confidential information, unexpected rewards, celebrity news, workplace rumors, or personal photographs. Humans are naturally curious, and attackers frequently use curiosity to entice victims into clicking links or downloading files. What appears to be an innocent opportunity to learn something interesting may actually serve as the entry point for a larger attack.

Trust-based social engineering attacks frequently involve impersonation. Attackers may pretend to be friends, coworkers, supervisors, family members, technical support agents, or representatives of trusted organizations. Social media platforms provide attackers with access to significant amounts of personal information that can be used to make impersonation attempts appear more convincing. The more information attackers possess, the easier it becomes to create believable stories.

Mobile application scams have become increasingly sophisticated. Cybercriminals create fraudulent applications that mimic legitimate services. These fake apps may resemble banking platforms, social media services, shopping applications, cryptocurrency wallets, productivity tools, or popular games. The goal is to persuade users to install the software and provide sensitive information. In some cases, the application functions partially as advertised while secretly collecting data or installing malware.

Fake customer support scams represent another growing threat. Victims may receive messages claiming that assistance is required to resolve account issues, process refunds, or restore access to services. Attackers often direct victims to call fraudulent support numbers or communicate through messaging platforms. During these interactions, victims may be persuaded to reveal credentials, install remote access software, or authorize transactions.

QR code scams have become more common as mobile payments and digital interactions increase. Cybercriminals create malicious QR codes that direct users to phishing websites or initiate unwanted downloads. Because QR codes conceal destination URLs, users cannot easily verify where they will be directed before scanning. This lack of visibility makes QR codes attractive tools for attackers.

Business email compromise attacks demonstrate how social engineering can target organizations as well as individuals. Attackers impersonate executives, managers, vendors, or trusted partners to request payments, sensitive information, or account changes. Mobile devices increase the effectiveness of these attacks because employees often review messages quickly while away from their desks. Limited visibility and rushed decision-making create favorable conditions for attackers.

One of the most important defenses against phishing and social engineering is verification. Whenever a message requests sensitive information, financial transactions, password changes, or urgent action, users should independently verify the request through trusted channels. Rather than clicking links provided in messages, users should visit official websites directly or contact organizations using verified contact information.

Awareness training plays a critical role in defense. Understanding how attackers operate allows users to recognize suspicious patterns. Common warning signs include unexpected requests, poor grammar, generic greetings, emotional manipulation, unfamiliar senders, unusual URLs, and requests for confidential information. While sophisticated attacks may avoid some of these indicators, many phishing attempts still reveal clues upon careful examination.

Multifactor authentication provides an additional layer of protection. Even if attackers obtain credentials, they may be unable to access accounts without the second authentication factor. While not a complete solution, multifactor authentication significantly reduces the effectiveness of many phishing attacks.

Password managers can also improve security by helping users identify fraudulent websites. Because password managers associate credentials with specific domains, they typically will not automatically fill passwords on counterfeit websites. This behavior can serve as an early warning sign that a website may not be legitimate.

Reporting suspicious messages contributes to broader cybersecurity efforts. Organizations often use reported phishing attempts to improve defenses, block malicious domains, and warn other users. Prompt reporting can help prevent additional victims from falling for the same scam.

Developing a skeptical mindset is one of the most effective long-term defenses. Skepticism does not mean assuming every message is malicious. Instead, it involves evaluating unexpected requests carefully and recognizing that cybercriminals actively attempt to manipulate emotions and behavior. Users who pause before acting, verify information independently, and maintain awareness of common tactics are significantly less likely to become victims.

The most important lesson is that cybersecurity is not solely a technical challenge. Human decision-making plays a central role in security outcomes. By understanding phishing, social engineering, and mobile app scams, users can strengthen one of the most important security layers available: themselves. Knowledge, awareness, and careful judgment remain powerful defenses against even the most sophisticated psychological attacks.

Anthony was in the middle of a hectic day

Anthony managed operations for a growing construction company. His work required constant communication with suppliers, contractors, clients, and employees. As a result, his smartphone became his primary business tool. He responded to emails, approved invoices, reviewed project updates, and managed financial transactions throughout the day. Like many busy professionals, he often handled messages quickly between meetings and job site visits.

One Tuesday afternoon, Anthony received a text message that appeared to come from his company's bank. The message warned of suspicious activity involving a recent transaction and instructed him to verify account information immediately. A link was included, along with a warning that account access might be restricted if action was not taken within two hours.

Anthony was in the middle of a hectic day. Several projects were behind schedule, clients were requesting updates, and suppliers were waiting for payment approvals. Concerned about the possibility of a banking issue, he clicked the link without giving it much thought. The website that appeared looked identical to the bank's official login page. The logos, colors, and design were nearly perfect.

Without hesitation, Anthony entered his username and password. The site then requested a verification code sent to his phone. Moments later, he received a legitimate authentication code from the bank and entered it into the website. A loading screen appeared briefly before displaying an error message stating that the service was temporarily unavailable.

Assuming the website was experiencing technical difficulties, Anthony closed the browser and returned to work. What he did not realize was that the website had been created by cybercriminals. The attackers had captured both his credentials and authentication code in real time. Using this information, they immediately logged into his account and began initiating unauthorized transactions.

Fortunately, the bank's fraud monitoring systems detected unusual activity and temporarily suspended the transactions. The bank contacted Anthony directly using official channels. During the conversation, he learned that the text message had not originated from the bank at all. He had become the target of a sophisticated smishing attack.

Embarrassed and frustrated, Anthony wondered how he had fallen for the scam. The message looked professional, the website appeared authentic, and the timing felt plausible. A cybersecurity consultant later explained that the attackers had intentionally created urgency. Their goal was to prevent careful analysis by making Anthony feel that immediate action was necessary.

Determined to learn from the experience, Anthony began studying social engineering techniques. He discovered that attackers rarely rely solely on technology. Instead, they exploit emotions such as fear, urgency, trust, and curiosity. The attackers had not hacked his account directly. They had persuaded him to provide access voluntarily.

Several months later, Anthony received another suspicious message. This time, the sender claimed to be a delivery company attempting to verify shipping information for an expensive package. The message included a link and requested immediate confirmation. Remembering his previous experience, Anthony resisted the urge to click. Instead, he opened the delivery company's official application and checked his account directly. No shipment existed. The message was fraudulent.

As his awareness grew, Anthony began sharing cybersecurity lessons with his employees. During team meetings, he discussed phishing attacks, social engineering tactics, and mobile security best practices. He encouraged workers to verify unusual requests independently and report suspicious messages immediately. Over time, cybersecurity awareness became part of the company's culture.

One employee, Sarah, later received a phone call from someone claiming to be technical support for a software provider. The caller requested account credentials to resolve a supposed licensing issue. Because of the training Anthony had provided, Sarah declined the request and contacted the software company directly. The company confirmed that no support representative had called. Another attack had been prevented through awareness and verification.

As months passed, Anthony became increasingly confident in his ability to recognize suspicious activity. He understood that attackers would continue adapting their methods, but he also realized that many scams relied on predictable psychological techniques. By slowing down, verifying information, and resisting emotional pressure, he dramatically reduced his risk.

A year after the banking incident, Anthony reflected on the experience. Initially, he viewed cybersecurity as a technical field handled by specialists. Now he understood that security also depended heavily on human behavior. Technology provided valuable defenses, but informed decision-making remained equally important.

Anthony's story illustrates a critical reality of modern cybersecurity. Attackers often find it easier to manipulate people than to defeat sophisticated security systems. They exploit natural human tendencies, create believable scenarios, and encourage rapid action. Their success depends not on advanced hacking skills alone but on understanding psychology.

The lesson extends far beyond financial scams. Social engineering techniques appear in many forms, including phishing emails, fake support calls, fraudulent applications, social media messages, and impersonation attempts. Regardless of the specific method, the underlying objective remains the same: convincing victims to take actions that benefit attackers.

By understanding how social engineering works, Anthony transformed from a vulnerable target into a more informed and resilient user. His experience demonstrates that awareness, skepticism, and verification are among the strongest defenses available. Technology can help protect users, but knowledge empowers them to recognize threats before damage occurs.

As mobile devices continue playing larger roles in communication, business, and financial activities, phishing and social engineering attacks will remain persistent challenges. However, individuals who understand attacker tactics and maintain disciplined security habits can significantly reduce their exposure to these risks. The principles explored in this chapter provide a foundation for safer digital interactions and stronger defenses against one of the most effective forms of cybercrime.

Chapter 5

Mobile App Permissions, Privacy Risks, and Data Collection

One of the most overlooked areas of mobile security involves application permissions and the vast amount of personal data collected by modern mobile applications. Most smartphone users install applications quickly, approve permission requests without careful review, and rarely consider how much information is being shared. While many applications require access to certain device functions to operate properly, others request permissions that exceed their legitimate needs. Understanding how permissions work, what risks they create, and how data collection affects privacy is essential for maintaining control over personal information in today's digital world.

Every mobile application operates within a security framework established by the device's operating system. One of the primary functions of this framework is permission management. Permissions determine what resources and information an application can access. These resources may include cameras, microphones, contacts, location services, storage, calendars, text messages, call logs, Bluetooth connections, and other device features. Permissions help prevent applications from accessing sensitive information without user approval.

When permissions are used responsibly, they enhance both security and functionality. A navigation application, for example, requires access to location services to provide directions. A video conferencing application needs access to the camera and microphone. A messaging app requires access to contacts if users wish to connect with people already stored on their devices. In these situations, permissions support legitimate functionality and improve the user experience.

Problems arise when applications request permissions that are unnecessary for their stated purpose. A simple flashlight application generally does not require access to contacts, location data, or microphone recordings. A calculator application should not need permission to read text messages or access photos. Excessive permission requests may indicate poor privacy practices, aggressive data collection strategies, or potentially malicious intent. Users who approve permissions without careful evaluation may expose themselves to unnecessary risks.

Data has become one of the most valuable resources in the modern digital economy. Many companies generate revenue by collecting, analyzing, and monetizing user information.

Mobile applications provide access to enormous amounts of data, making smartphones powerful data collection platforms. Information gathered through applications may include demographics, browsing habits, purchasing behavior, location history, interests, social connections, device characteristics, and usage patterns. This information is often used for targeted advertising, analytics, personalization, and business intelligence.

Location tracking represents one of the most sensitive forms of data collection. Modern smartphones can determine precise geographic locations through GPS, Wi-Fi networks, Bluetooth signals, and cellular connections. Many applications request access to location data, even when location services are not essential to their core functionality. Continuous location tracking can reveal where users live, work, shop, exercise, travel, and spend time. Over extended periods, this information can create highly detailed profiles of individual behavior.

Some applications collect location information even when they are not actively being used. Background location tracking allows apps to continue gathering data while operating behind the scenes. Although certain services legitimately require this capability, users should carefully evaluate whether background location access is truly necessary. Limiting location permissions to "while using the app" can significantly improve privacy without sacrificing functionality.

Contact list access presents another significant privacy concern. Contacts contain valuable information about personal and professional relationships. When users grant contact permissions, applications may gain access to names, phone numbers, email addresses, and other details associated with individuals stored on the device. This creates privacy implications not only for the user but also for friends, family members, coworkers, and clients who may never have consented to data sharing.

Microphone and camera permissions deserve careful consideration because they provide access to highly sensitive information. Legitimate applications such as video conferencing platforms, voice messaging services, and photography tools require these permissions to function properly. However, excessive or unnecessary access may create opportunities for abuse. Although operating systems implement safeguards to prevent unauthorized surveillance, users should remain aware of which applications have access to recording capabilities.

Storage permissions allow applications to access files stored on devices. These files may include documents, photos, videos, downloads, and other personal content. Improperly secured applications or malicious software with storage access may expose sensitive information to unauthorized parties. Reviewing storage permissions periodically helps users maintain greater control over personal data.

Advertising identifiers represent another aspect of mobile privacy that many users overlook. Mobile operating systems assign unique advertising identifiers to devices, allowing advertisers to track user activity across applications and services. While these identifiers do not directly reveal names or contact information, they can be linked to detailed behavioral profiles. Many operating systems now provide options to limit advertising tracking or reset advertising identifiers, giving users greater control over data collection practices.

Application developers often incorporate third-party software development kits, commonly known as SDKs, into their products. These SDKs provide functionality such as analytics, advertising, payment processing, and social media integration. However, third-party components may collect information independently of the application itself. As a result, user data may be shared with multiple organizations rather than remaining solely with the app developer. Understanding the role of third-party SDKs highlights the complexity of modern data collection ecosystems.

Privacy policies are intended to inform users about data collection practices. Unfortunately, many privacy policies are lengthy, complex, and difficult to understand. As a result, users frequently accept terms without reviewing them. While reading every privacy policy may be impractical, examining key sections related to data collection, sharing practices, retention periods, and user rights can provide valuable insights into how information will be handled.

Behavioral profiling has become increasingly sophisticated. By combining information from multiple sources, organizations can develop detailed profiles of users' interests, habits, preferences, routines, and behaviors. These profiles may be used for advertising, content recommendations, product development, risk assessments, and other purposes. While personalization can improve user experiences, it also raises important questions about privacy, transparency, and informed consent.

Cybercriminals also recognize the value of personal data. Applications that collect large amounts of information become attractive targets for attackers. Data breaches involving mobile applications can expose personal details, financial information, credentials, and behavioral data. Even organizations with strong security programs occasionally experience breaches. Limiting unnecessary data sharing reduces potential exposure if a security incident occurs.

Permission abuse can occur when legitimate applications use approved permissions in unexpected ways. An application may technically comply with permission requirements while collecting more information than users anticipate. For example, access to motion sensors, device identifiers, and network information may reveal behavioral patterns without directly accessing traditional personal data. Understanding that permissions often provide broader access than expected encourages more thoughtful decision-making.

Regular permission reviews are an important security habit. Most mobile operating systems provide tools that allow users to review which applications have access to specific resources. Periodically examining these settings helps identify unnecessary permissions and remove access that is no longer required. Many users discover applications retaining permissions long after they stop using related features.

The principle of least privilege is a valuable concept in cybersecurity. This principle states that applications should receive only the permissions necessary to perform their intended functions. By limiting access, users reduce potential risks associated with misuse, compromise, or unauthorized data collection. Applying this principle consistently strengthens both privacy and security.

Modern operating systems have introduced enhanced privacy controls to help users manage permissions more effectively. Temporary permissions, one-time location access, permission reminders, privacy dashboards, and activity indicators provide greater transparency. These tools empower users to make informed decisions and monitor how applications interact with sensitive resources.

Ultimately, protecting privacy requires active participation. Technology companies provide controls and settings, but users must choose how to apply them. Understanding permissions, evaluating requests carefully, reviewing access regularly, and maintaining awareness of data collection practices help individuals retain greater control over their digital lives.

As mobile devices continue evolving, data collection will likely become even more sophisticated. New sensors, services, and technologies will create additional opportunities for both innovation and privacy concerns. Users who understand how permissions and data collection work will be better prepared to navigate this evolving landscape while protecting their personal information and maintaining greater digital autonomy.

Rachel watched a documentary about digital privacy

Rachel considered herself a careful smartphone user. She avoided suspicious websites, kept her operating system updated, and downloaded applications only from official app stores. Because she followed these basic security practices, she believed her personal information was relatively safe. What she did not realize was how much data she was voluntarily sharing through everyday applications.

Rachel worked as a fitness coach and used numerous mobile apps throughout her day. She tracked workouts, communicated with clients, managed appointments, monitored nutrition, shared content on social media, and used navigation services while traveling between training locations. Each application requested permissions during installation, and like most users, Rachel usually approved them without much thought.

One weekend, Rachel watched a documentary about digital privacy. The program discussed how mobile applications collect and share user information. Curious, she decided to review the permissions on her smartphone. What she discovered surprised her.

A weather application had access to her location at all times. A simple puzzle game had permission to access contacts and storage. Several shopping applications retained location access even though she rarely used them. Multiple social media apps had access to her microphone, camera, contacts, and photo library. The sheer number of permissions granted over time was far greater than she expected.

Determined to learn more, Rachel began researching how mobile applications collect data. She discovered that many apps gather information not only for functionality but also for analytics, advertising, and personalization purposes. Some applications shared information with third-party partners, while others combined data from multiple sources to create behavioral profiles. The realization made her reconsider how she approached privacy.

Over the next few weeks, Rachel carefully reviewed each application installed on her device. She removed apps she no longer used and adjusted permissions to align with actual needs. Location access was restricted to "while using the app" whenever possible. Microphone and camera permissions were disabled for applications that did not require them. Contact access was removed from services that had no legitimate need for her address book.

As Rachel made these changes, she began noticing improvements. Some applications displayed fewer personalized advertisements. Others requested permissions again when attempting to access certain features, allowing her to evaluate requests more carefully. Most importantly, she felt more informed and in control of her information.

Several months later, a popular fitness application experienced a major data breach. Millions of user records were exposed, including profile information, workout histories, and location data. Because Rachel had previously limited the amount of information shared through the platform, her exposure was significantly reduced. Many users affected by the breach had provided extensive personal details that were now potentially available to attackers.

The incident reinforced Rachel's belief that privacy decisions matter. While users cannot eliminate all risks, they can influence how much information becomes available if a security incident occurs. Every piece of unnecessary data shared creates additional exposure.

Rachel soon began discussing privacy with her clients. During training sessions, conversations occasionally shifted toward technology and mobile apps. Many clients assumed privacy settings were too complicated or unimportant. Rachel shared her experiences and demonstrated how permission reviews could be completed in just a few minutes. Several clients were surprised to discover how much access various applications possessed.

One client, Daniel, found that a flashlight app on his phone had permission to access location services, contacts, and storage. Another discovered multiple applications collecting location information continuously in the background. These discoveries helped people understand that privacy is not solely about preventing cybercrime. It is also about maintaining control over personal information.

As Rachel continued learning about cybersecurity, she encountered the principle of least privilege. The concept immediately resonated with her. She realized that permissions should be granted intentionally rather than automatically. Applications should receive only what they truly need to function. This simple idea became the foundation of her approach to mobile privacy.

A year after reviewing her permissions for the first time, Rachel looked back on how much her perspective had changed. She still used mobile applications extensively, but she approached them differently. Instead of assuming every request was reasonable, she evaluated permissions thoughtfully. Instead of accepting data collection as unavoidable, she actively managed privacy settings and reviewed access regularly.

Rachel's experience demonstrates an important lesson for modern smartphone users. Privacy risks often emerge not from dramatic cyberattacks but from routine decisions made every day. Small permission approvals accumulate over time, creating extensive access to personal information. Understanding these risks empowers users to make better choices.

Her story also highlights the value of awareness. Before watching the documentary, Rachel had no reason to question the permissions she granted. Like many people, she assumed that applications would only request what they needed. Education changed that assumption and encouraged more thoughtful behavior. Knowledge transformed her from a passive participant into an active manager of her digital privacy.

The lessons Rachel learned apply to anyone who uses mobile technology. Permissions exist for a reason, but they require careful evaluation. Data collection supports many useful services, but users should understand what information is being gathered and why. Privacy is not about avoiding technology; it is about using technology responsibly and intentionally.

As mobile devices become increasingly integrated into daily life, privacy will remain a critical issue. New applications, services, and connected technologies will continue generating vast amounts of information. Individuals who understand permissions, data collection, and privacy controls will be better equipped to protect themselves and maintain greater control over their digital identities.

Rachel's journey illustrates that meaningful privacy improvements do not require advanced technical expertise. They begin with awareness, thoughtful decision-making, and a willingness to review the settings that shape how information is shared. These habits create stronger privacy protections and contribute to a more secure and informed digital experience.

services, but users should understand what information is being gathered and why. Privacy is not about avoiding technology; it is about using technology responsibly and intentionally.

As mobile devices become increasingly integrated into daily life, privacy will remain a critical issue. New applications, sensors, and connected technologies will continue generating vast amounts of information. Individuals who understand permissions, data collection, and privacy controls will be better equipped to protect themselves and maintain greater control over their digital identities.

Rachel's journey illustrates that meaningful privacy improvements do not require advanced technical expertise. They begin with awareness, thoughtful decision-making, and a willingness to review the settings that shape how information is shared. These habits create stronger privacy protections and contribute to a more secure and informed digital experience.

Chapter 6

Defending Against Mobile App Attacks and Building a Personal Security Strategy

Understanding how cybercriminals attack mobile applications is only half of the cybersecurity equation. The other half involves building effective defenses. While no security system can guarantee complete protection against every threat, users who adopt strong security habits significantly reduce their risk of becoming victims. Mobile security is not achieved through a single application, setting, or tool. Instead, it results from multiple layers of protection working together. This chapter explores how individuals can develop a comprehensive personal security strategy to defend against mobile app attacks and maintain long-term digital safety.

One of the most important principles in cybersecurity is defense in depth. Defense in depth refers to the use of multiple security controls that work together to protect devices, accounts, and information. If one layer fails, other layers continue providing protection. For example, even if a password is compromised, multifactor authentication may prevent unauthorized access. If malware reaches a device, operating system protections and security software may limit its impact. Layered security reduces the likelihood that a single mistake or vulnerability will result in a major compromise.

The foundation of any mobile security strategy begins with maintaining control over the device itself. Physical security remains important even in an increasingly digital world. Smartphones should be protected with strong screen locks such as PINs, passwords, biometric authentication, or combinations of these methods. Devices left unlocked create opportunities for unauthorized access, especially if lost, stolen, or temporarily unattended. A secure lock screen serves as the first line of defense against many threats.

Strong authentication practices extend beyond the device lock screen. Every important account should be protected with unique, complex passwords. Password reuse remains one of the most common security mistakes. When the same password is used across multiple services, a compromise affecting one account can lead to compromises elsewhere. Cybercriminals frequently use credential stuffing attacks, where stolen usernames and passwords are automatically tested against numerous services. Unique passwords limit the effectiveness of these attacks.

Password managers provide a practical solution to the challenge of maintaining strong credentials. Rather than relying on memory, password managers generate and store unique passwords for each account. This allows users to create highly secure credentials without sacrificing convenience. Password managers also help identify fraudulent websites by only filling credentials on recognized domains. Their use significantly strengthens overall account security.

Multifactor authentication, often abbreviated as MFA, is one of the most effective security controls available. MFA requires users to provide two or more forms of verification before accessing an account. Common factors include passwords, authentication applications, biometric data, hardware tokens, or one-time verification codes. Even if attackers obtain a password, they often cannot access the account without the additional authentication factor. Whenever possible, MFA should be enabled on financial accounts, email services, social media platforms, cloud storage services, and other important systems.

Software updates play a critical role in mobile security. Developers continuously identify vulnerabilities and release patches to address them. Delaying updates leaves devices exposed to known weaknesses that attackers may exploit. Many cyberattacks succeed because users continue operating outdated software long after fixes become available. Automatic updates help ensure that security patches are applied promptly and consistently.

Application management is another essential component of mobile defense. Users should download software only from trusted sources such as official app stores. While official stores are not immune to malicious applications, they generally provide significantly greater protection than unofficial marketplaces. Before installing software, users should review developer information, ratings, reviews, download counts, and permission requests. Careful evaluation reduces the likelihood of installing malicious or poorly secured applications.

Permission management remains one of the most powerful privacy and security tools available to users. Applications should receive access only to resources necessary for their intended functions. Excessive permissions increase risk by expanding the amount of information available to applications. Regular permission reviews help identify unnecessary access and ensure that applications operate according to user expectations.

Network security is another important aspect of mobile protection. Smartphones frequently connect to public Wi-Fi networks in airports, hotels, restaurants, cafes, and other public locations. While convenient, public networks may expose users to additional risks. Attackers sometimes create fake hotspots designed to intercept communications or collect credentials. Using virtual private networks, commonly known as VPNs, can help protect data transmitted over untrusted networks by encrypting communications between devices and remote servers.

Encryption plays a central role in modern cybersecurity. Encryption transforms information into unreadable formats that can only be accessed using appropriate keys. Most modern smartphones support device encryption by default. Encryption protects data stored on devices and helps prevent unauthorized access if a device is lost or stolen. Users should verify that encryption features remain enabled and understand how they contribute to overall security.

Backup strategies provide protection against data loss resulting from malware, ransomware, hardware failure, theft, or accidental deletion. Important information should be backed up regularly using trusted cloud services or secure local storage solutions. Effective backups ensure that users can recover data even if devices become compromised or unavailable. The ability to restore information quickly can significantly reduce the impact of security incidents.

Security awareness remains one of the most valuable defenses available. Cybercriminals frequently target human behavior through phishing, social engineering, impersonation attacks, and scams. Users who understand common attack techniques are better equipped to recognize suspicious activity and avoid dangerous situations. Security awareness is not a one-time activity but an ongoing process of learning and adaptation.

Recognizing warning signs of compromise helps users respond quickly when problems occur. Common indicators include unexpected battery drain, unusual device heating, excessive data usage, unfamiliar applications, unauthorized account activity, unexpected advertisements, performance issues, and suspicious permission requests. While these symptoms do not always indicate malicious activity, they warrant investigation. Early detection often limits the damage caused by security incidents.

Incident response planning is another valuable component of personal security. Many individuals never consider what they would do if a device became compromised. Preparing in advance allows for faster and more effective responses. Important steps may include changing passwords, revoking access tokens, contacting financial institutions, reporting fraud, restoring backups, and seeking professional assistance.

A prepared response can significantly reduce recovery time and financial losses.

Identity protection has become increasingly important as cybercriminals focus on personal information. Monitoring financial accounts, reviewing credit reports, enabling account alerts, and verifying suspicious communications help reduce identity theft risks. Early detection of unauthorized activity often prevents larger problems from developing.

Mobile security also involves protecting family members and other device users. Children, teenagers, and less experienced users may be particularly vulnerable to scams, phishing attempts, and malicious applications. Sharing knowledge and encouraging safe practices contributes to stronger security for entire households. Security is often most effective when approached as a shared responsibility rather than an individual concern.

Privacy considerations should be incorporated into every security strategy. Limiting unnecessary data sharing reduces exposure to both cybercriminals and data collection practices. Users should regularly review privacy settings, advertising preferences, application permissions, and account configurations. Maintaining greater control over personal information strengthens both privacy and security outcomes.

As technology continues evolving, new threats will emerge alongside new defenses. Artificial intelligence, connected devices, wearable technology, digital payments, and advanced communication systems will create both opportunities and challenges. Users who adopt flexible security mindsets will be better prepared to adapt to changing conditions. Continuous learning remains one of the most important long-term cybersecurity investments.

A personal security strategy should be realistic and sustainable. Complex security measures that are difficult to maintain often fail over time. Effective security balances protection, usability, and convenience. The goal is not to eliminate every possible risk but to reduce exposure significantly while maintaining productive use of technology. Consistency is often more valuable than complexity.

Ultimately, cybersecurity is about managing risk. Every decision involves tradeoffs between convenience and protection. Users who understand these tradeoffs can make informed choices aligned with their personal needs and priorities. Security is not a destination but an ongoing process of awareness, adaptation, and improvement.

The lessons throughout this book emphasize that individuals are not powerless against cyber threats. By understanding attacker techniques, adopting strong defensive practices, and maintaining a proactive mindset, users can dramatically improve their security posture. Building a personal security strategy empowers individuals to navigate the digital world with greater confidence, resilience, and control.

Marcus enabled multifactor authentication

Marcus had always considered himself lucky when it came to technology. He had never experienced a major cyberattack, never lost important data, and never dealt with identity theft. Because nothing serious had happened, he rarely thought about cybersecurity. His smartphone contained banking applications, business accounts, family photographs, personal documents, and years of communications. Despite the value of this information, security was not something he actively managed.

One evening, Marcus attended a community seminar on digital safety. The speaker discussed mobile app threats, phishing attacks, malware, identity theft, and personal security strategies. Throughout the presentation, Marcus realized how vulnerable he actually was. He used the same password on several accounts, had not reviewed app permissions in years, rarely updated certain applications, and frequently connected to public Wi-Fi networks without considering the risks.

The seminar motivated him to evaluate his security practices. The following weekend, Marcus dedicated several hours to reviewing his smartphone and online accounts. He started by creating unique passwords for important services and installing a password manager. Although the process required some effort, he quickly appreciated the convenience of having secure credentials stored safely.

Next, Marcus enabled multifactor authentication wherever possible. His email accounts, banking services, cloud storage platforms, and social media profiles all received additional layers of protection. He realized that even if a password were stolen, attackers would face significant obstacles accessing his accounts.

As he continued reviewing his device, Marcus discovered numerous applications he no longer used. Some retained access to contacts, location services, microphones, and storage. He removed unnecessary apps and adjusted permissions for the remaining ones. The process gave him a greater sense of control over his personal information.

Several months later, Marcus received an email appearing to come from a popular cloud storage provider. The message claimed that unusual activity had been detected and requested immediate password verification. Before attending the seminar, Marcus probably would have clicked the link without hesitation. Instead, he paused and evaluated the situation carefully.

The message created urgency, contained a suspicious web address, and requested sensitive information. Rather than using the provided link, Marcus visited the service's official website directly. No security alert existed. The email was fraudulent. His awareness prevented him from becoming a victim.

Not long afterward, Marcus encountered another situation that tested his preparedness. While traveling for business, he accidentally left his smartphone in a taxi. Initially, panic set in. The device contained valuable information and access to numerous accounts. However, because he had developed a personal security strategy, he knew exactly what to do.

Using a trusted computer, Marcus accessed his device management account and located the phone remotely. He activated lost mode, preventing unauthorized access. Because device encryption and strong authentication were already enabled, he felt confident that his information remained protected. Within a few hours, the taxi company recovered the phone and returned it to him.

The experience reinforced the value of preparation. Marcus realized that security measures are most effective when implemented before problems occur. Waiting until after an incident often limits available options. By planning ahead, he had transformed a potentially serious situation into a manageable inconvenience.

Inspired by his progress, Marcus began sharing cybersecurity lessons with his family. His teenage daughter frequently downloaded applications without reviewing permissions. His parents often responded to suspicious emails and text messages. Rather than criticizing their habits, Marcus explained common risks and demonstrated practical safety measures. Together, they reviewed privacy settings, enabled multifactor authentication, and discussed phishing tactics.

Several months later, Marcus's father received a phone call from someone claiming to represent a government agency. The caller demanded immediate payment for an alleged legal issue and threatened severe consequences if action was not taken. Remembering earlier conversations, his father refused to provide information and verified the claim independently. The call was a scam. Awareness and preparation had prevented another potential victim.

As the years passed, cybersecurity became a routine part of Marcus's life rather than an occasional concern. He reviewed permissions regularly, maintained backups, installed updates promptly, monitored account activity, and remained alert for suspicious communications. These habits required minimal effort once they became established. More importantly, they provided ongoing protection against a wide variety of threats.

Marcus eventually realized that cybersecurity was not about fear. It was about confidence. Understanding risks allowed him to use technology more effectively because he knew how to protect himself. Rather than worrying constantly about threats, he focused on maintaining good habits and responding thoughtfully to unusual situations.

One day, a colleague experienced a ransomware attack that encrypted years of business records. The incident caused significant disruption because no recent backups existed. Marcus sympathized with the situation but also recognized how his own backup strategy would help him recover more quickly under similar circumstances. The experience reinforced the importance of proactive preparation.

Looking back, Marcus understood that the most important change had occurred in his mindset. Before learning about cybersecurity, he assumed security was someone else's responsibility. Now he recognized that individuals play a critical role in protecting their own information. Technology companies provide tools and safeguards, but users must choose how to apply them.

Marcus's journey demonstrates that effective mobile security does not require advanced technical expertise. It begins with awareness, practical habits, and a willingness to take responsibility for personal protection. Small improvements accumulate over time, creating meaningful reductions in risk. Strong passwords, multifactor authentication, permission management, backups, updates, and security awareness work together to form a resilient defense system.

His story also highlights the value of preparation. Security incidents often occur unexpectedly, but their impact can be reduced significantly when users have planned ahead. Whether facing phishing attacks, lost devices, malware infections, or identity theft attempts, preparation provides options and improves outcomes.

As mobile technology continues evolving, the principles Marcus adopted remain relevant. Threats will change, tools will improve, and new challenges will emerge. However, the foundation of effective security remains constant: awareness, vigilance, preparation, and continuous learning. Users who embrace these principles position themselves to navigate the digital world safely and confidently.

The lessons in this chapter represent the culmination of the defensive strategies explored throughout this book. By understanding threats, implementing safeguards, and maintaining a proactive security mindset, individuals can dramatically strengthen their defenses against mobile app attacks. Cybersecurity is ultimately about empowerment—giving users the knowledge and tools needed to protect themselves, their information, and their digital future.

Chapter 7

Future Mobile Threats and Staying Secure in an Evolving Digital World

Mobile cybersecurity is not a static field. The threats that exist today will continue evolving as technology advances, user behavior changes, and cybercriminals develop new attack methods. Understanding current threats is important, but preparing for future risks is equally critical. Smartphones are becoming increasingly integrated into nearly every aspect of daily life, from banking and healthcare to transportation, communication, entertainment, education, and business. As mobile devices become more powerful and interconnected, they will continue attracting the attention of cybercriminals seeking new opportunities for profit, espionage, fraud, and disruption.

One of the most important realities of cybersecurity is that attackers constantly adapt. Every time a new security control is introduced, cybercriminals begin searching for methods to bypass it. When organizations improve authentication systems, attackers develop more sophisticated phishing campaigns. When operating systems strengthen malware defenses, attackers create new delivery techniques. This ongoing cycle of attack and defense has existed since the earliest days of computing and will continue into the future. Users who understand this dynamic are better prepared to adapt their security practices over time.

Artificial intelligence is expected to play a major role in the future of mobile cybersecurity. AI technologies offer tremendous benefits, including improved threat detection, automated analysis, and enhanced security monitoring. However, cybercriminals also use artificial intelligence to improve attacks. AI can generate highly convincing phishing messages, automate reconnaissance activities, identify vulnerabilities, create realistic voice impersonations, and personalize scams at unprecedented scales. The same technology that helps defenders can also strengthen attacker capabilities.

One emerging concern involves AI-generated social engineering attacks. Traditional phishing campaigns often contain grammatical errors, awkward wording, or generic messages. AI systems can now produce highly convincing communications that closely resemble legitimate correspondence. Attackers may use information gathered from social media, public records, and previous breaches to create personalized messages that appear authentic. As these technologies improve, users must become increasingly vigilant when evaluating digital communications.

Deepfake technology represents another growing challenge. Deepfakes use artificial intelligence to generate realistic audio, video, and images that imitate real individuals. Cybercriminals may use deepfakes to impersonate executives, family members, customer service representatives, or public officials. Imagine receiving a video call that appears to come from a trusted colleague or hearing a voice message that sounds exactly like a family member requesting urgent assistance. These scenarios are becoming increasingly realistic as AI-generated media improves.

Mobile payment systems will likely remain attractive targets for cybercriminals. As societies continue shifting toward digital transactions, mobile wallets, contactless payments, cryptocurrency platforms, and online banking services will become even more central to daily life. Attackers are expected to focus significant resources on compromising financial applications, stealing credentials, intercepting transactions, and exploiting weaknesses within payment ecosystems. Users who rely heavily on mobile financial services should prioritize strong authentication and account monitoring practices.

The growth of cryptocurrency and decentralized finance applications introduces additional security considerations. Cryptocurrency transactions are often irreversible, making them attractive targets for attackers. Mobile cryptocurrency wallets, exchanges, and investment platforms store valuable assets that may be difficult to recover if stolen. Users engaging with digital currencies should understand the unique security challenges associated with managing private keys, securing wallets, and identifying fraudulent investment schemes.

The Internet of Things, commonly referred to as IoT, will further expand the mobile threat landscape. Smartphones increasingly serve as control centers for connected devices such as smart home systems, security cameras, appliances, wearable technology, vehicles, and healthcare equipment. While these technologies provide convenience and automation, they also create additional attack surfaces. A compromised smartphone may potentially provide access to multiple connected systems, increasing the consequences of a successful attack.

Wearable technology continues growing in popularity. Smartwatches, fitness trackers, health monitors, and other wearable devices collect large amounts of personal information. These devices often synchronize data with smartphones and cloud services. As wearable technology becomes more advanced, protecting the information generated by these devices will become increasingly important. Health data, location information, activity records, and biometric measurements represent highly sensitive information that may attract both commercial and criminal interest.

Biometric authentication technologies are expected to become even more widespread. Fingerprint recognition, facial recognition, voice recognition, and behavioral biometrics offer convenient alternatives to traditional passwords. While biometrics provide significant security benefits, they also introduce unique challenges. Unlike passwords, biometric identifiers cannot easily be changed if compromised. Future security systems will likely combine biometric authentication with additional factors to strengthen overall protection.

Cloud computing will continue shaping the future of mobile technology. Many applications rely heavily on cloud services for storage, processing, synchronization, and collaboration. While cloud infrastructure often provides strong security controls, users must still understand how data is stored, shared, and protected. Future security strategies will increasingly focus on securing interactions between devices, cloud platforms, and connected services.

Privacy concerns will remain central to discussions about mobile technology. As applications collect more data and analytical capabilities improve, questions about surveillance, profiling, consent, and transparency will become increasingly important. Organizations may gain deeper insights into user behavior through advanced analytics and machine learning. Users who understand privacy principles and actively manage their information will be better positioned to protect their digital identities.

Quantum computing represents a long-term consideration for cybersecurity professionals. Although practical large-scale quantum computers remain under development, their eventual arrival could affect many existing encryption methods. Researchers are already working on quantum-resistant cryptographic techniques designed to protect future communications and data. While quantum computing does not present an immediate threat to most users, it highlights the importance of adapting security practices as technology evolves.

Mobile operating systems will continue introducing new security features designed to address emerging threats. Enhanced sandboxing, improved permission controls, stronger encryption, advanced malware detection, privacy dashboards, and AI-driven protections are likely to become more common. Users should take advantage of these improvements by keeping devices updated and learning how new security features work.

Cybersecurity awareness will remain one of the most valuable defenses available. Technology can provide powerful protections, but informed users play a critical role in identifying suspicious activity and making safe decisions. Attackers often focus on human behavior because technical defenses continue improving. Education, awareness, and critical thinking therefore remain essential components of long-term security.

The concept of digital resilience is becoming increasingly important. Digital resilience refers to the ability to prepare for, respond to, and recover from cybersecurity incidents. Rather than assuming attacks can be prevented entirely, resilient individuals and organizations recognize that incidents may occur and develop strategies to minimize their impact. Backups, incident response plans, account recovery procedures, and security awareness all contribute to resilience.

Maintaining a security mindset is perhaps the most important long-term strategy. A security mindset involves questioning unexpected requests, verifying information independently, evaluating risks thoughtfully, and remaining aware of potential threats. Users with strong security mindsets are less likely to act impulsively and more likely to recognize suspicious situations. This mindset remains valuable regardless of how technology changes.

Continuous learning is another essential habit. Cybersecurity evolves rapidly, and new threats emerge regularly. Staying informed about security developments, reviewing best practices, and adapting to changing conditions help users maintain effective defenses. Learning does not require becoming a technical expert. Even basic awareness of current trends can significantly improve security outcomes.

The future of mobile cybersecurity will undoubtedly bring both challenges and opportunities. New technologies will create innovative services, greater convenience, and expanded capabilities. At the same time, cybercriminals will continue searching for weaknesses to exploit. The goal is not to fear technological progress but to approach it responsibly. Understanding risks and implementing appropriate safeguards allows users to enjoy the benefits of innovation while minimizing exposure to threats.

Ultimately, cybersecurity is a journey rather than a destination. No single solution will remain effective forever. Success depends on adaptability, awareness, preparation, and a willingness to learn. Users who embrace these principles will be better equipped to navigate an increasingly connected world and protect themselves against both current and future threats.

The lessons throughout this book provide a foundation for building stronger security habits and making informed decisions. While the specific threats may change over time, the underlying principles of awareness, verification, layered defenses, and responsible technology use will remain valuable. By applying these principles consistently, individuals can strengthen their resilience and maintain greater control over their digital lives.

Ethan attended a cybersecurity conference

Ethan had always been fascinated by technology. As a software consultant, he followed developments in artificial intelligence, cloud computing, digital payments, and mobile applications closely. He enjoyed experimenting with new technologies and often adopted innovative services long before most people. His enthusiasm helped him stay ahead professionally, but it also exposed him to new risks.

One year, Ethan attended a cybersecurity conference focused on emerging threats. Experts discussed artificial intelligence, deepfake technology, advanced phishing campaigns, cryptocurrency security, and the future of mobile devices. The presentations were both exciting and concerning. Ethan realized that the cybersecurity landscape was changing rapidly, and many traditional assumptions about trust and verification were becoming less reliable.

Several months after the conference, Ethan experienced an incident that reinforced these lessons. One evening, he received a voicemail that sounded exactly like his younger brother. The message explained that an emergency had occurred while traveling overseas and requested immediate financial assistance. The voice sounded authentic. The details seemed plausible. Under normal circumstances, Ethan might have acted immediately.

However, he remembered a conference presentation about AI-generated voice cloning. Rather than sending money, Ethan contacted his brother through a separate communication channel. To his surprise, his brother was safe at home and had never made the call. The voicemail had been generated using publicly available recordings from social media videos and online content. The attackers had used artificial intelligence to create a convincing impersonation.

The experience left a strong impression. Ethan realized that future attacks might not contain obvious warning signs. Traditional indicators such as poor grammar or suspicious wording were becoming less reliable. Cybercriminals now possessed tools capable of producing highly realistic communications. Verification had become more important than ever.

Determined to strengthen his defenses, Ethan began reviewing his digital habits. He updated account recovery procedures, enabled additional authentication measures, and discussed verification strategies with family members. Together, they established simple methods for confirming urgent requests involving money, sensitive information, or unusual circumstances. These precautions provided additional protection against impersonation attempts.

Not long afterward, Ethan purchased several smart home devices, including security cameras, lighting controls, and environmental sensors. The convenience was impressive. He could monitor his home remotely, automate daily routines, and receive alerts through his smartphone. At the same time, he recognized that every connected device introduced additional security considerations.

Rather than rushing through setup processes, Ethan carefully reviewed security settings. Default passwords were replaced with strong credentials. Multifactor authentication was enabled wherever available. Firmware updates were installed promptly. Network segmentation was used to separate smart devices from more sensitive systems. These measures required some effort, but they significantly improved security.

As artificial intelligence tools became more common, Ethan noticed changes in phishing attempts. Messages were becoming more personalized and convincing. Some referenced specific projects, interests, or recent activities. Rather than relying solely on technological defenses, he developed a habit of slowing down whenever communications involved urgency or requests for sensitive information. This simple practice prevented several potential mistakes.

One day, a colleague named Sarah contacted Ethan about a suspicious message she had received. The email appeared to come from her company's chief executive officer and requested immediate approval of a financial transaction. Everything about the message seemed legitimate. The writing style matched previous communications, and the timing aligned with an ongoing project.

Ethan suggested verifying the request through another channel before taking action. Sarah called the executive directly and discovered that the message was fraudulent. Attackers had used artificial intelligence to analyze previous communications and generate a highly convincing impersonation. Because she verified the request independently, the attack failed.

The incident reinforced Ethan's belief that human judgment remained essential despite technological advances. Artificial intelligence could generate realistic content, but it could not eliminate the value of verification, skepticism, and critical thinking. Technology would continue evolving, but fundamental security principles remained relevant.

Over the years, Ethan continued adapting his security strategy. He stayed informed about emerging threats, reviewed security settings regularly, and remained cautious when adopting new technologies. Rather than viewing cybersecurity as a collection of technical tools, he saw it as an ongoing process of awareness and adaptation.

His perspective influenced those around him. Friends, family members, and coworkers often sought his advice regarding security questions. Rather than overwhelming them with technical details, Ethan emphasized practical habits: verify unexpected requests, use multifactor authentication, maintain backups, review permissions, install updates, and remain alert for unusual activity. These recommendations were simple, but they addressed many of the most common risks.

As the digital world became increasingly complex, Ethan noticed a pattern. The individuals who experienced the fewest security problems were not necessarily the most technically skilled. Instead, they were the ones who consistently applied good habits and maintained awareness. Security success often depended more on behavior than technical expertise.

Years later, Ethan reflected on everything he had learned. Technology had changed dramatically. Artificial intelligence, smart devices, advanced biometrics, and digital financial systems had become deeply integrated into daily life. Yet the core principles of cybersecurity remained surprisingly consistent. Awareness, preparation, verification, and adaptability continued serving as reliable foundations for personal security.

Ethan understood that future threats would continue emerging. New technologies would create opportunities for innovation as well as exploitation. However, he no longer viewed these developments with fear. Instead, he approached them with informed caution and confidence. Knowledge provided perspective, and preparation provided resilience.

His journey illustrates an important lesson for anyone navigating the modern digital world. Cybersecurity is not about predicting every possible threat. It is about building habits and strategies that remain effective even as conditions change. Users who cultivate awareness, embrace continuous learning, and adapt thoughtfully to new technologies position themselves for long-term success.

The story of Ethan serves as a reminder that the future of cybersecurity belongs not only to technology companies, governments, or security professionals. Every smartphone user plays a role in protecting their information and shaping their digital experience. By applying the principles explored throughout this book, individuals can strengthen their defenses, improve their resilience, and confidently embrace the opportunities offered by an increasingly connected world.

As you conclude this book, remember that cybersecurity is an ongoing journey. The threats will evolve, the technologies will change, and new challenges will emerge. However, the knowledge, awareness, and habits developed through continuous learning will remain powerful tools for protecting yourself and those around you. With preparation, vigilance, and adaptability, you can navigate the future securely and confidently.

Chapter 8

Incident Response and Recovery After a Mobile Security Breach

No matter how careful a person may be, no mobile security strategy can guarantee complete protection against every threat. Cybercriminals continuously develop new attack techniques, software vulnerabilities occasionally emerge, and human mistakes sometimes occur despite the best intentions. For this reason, one of the most important aspects of cybersecurity is understanding how to respond when a security incident occurs. The ability to react quickly, limit damage, recover effectively, and learn from the experience can significantly reduce the long-term impact of a breach. In many cases, the difference between a minor inconvenience and a major disaster depends on how the victim responds during the first hours after discovering a problem.

A security incident occurs whenever a device, application, account, or piece of information is accessed, altered, stolen, exposed, or disrupted without authorization. Mobile security incidents may include malware infections, stolen credentials, compromised accounts, unauthorized financial transactions, data breaches, spyware infections, ransomware attacks, lost devices, stolen smartphones, and social engineering scams.

While each incident is unique, most response efforts follow a similar set of principles designed to contain the threat and restore security.

The first step in incident response is recognizing that an incident may have occurred. Many users fail to notice early warning signs because they assume unusual behavior has harmless explanations. Common indicators of compromise include unexpected battery drain, unusual device heating, increased data usage, unfamiliar applications, strange pop-up messages, unauthorized transactions, unexpected password reset notifications, login alerts from unfamiliar locations, changes to account settings, or messages sent without the user's knowledge. Recognizing these indicators quickly allows users to take action before attackers cause additional damage.

Once suspicious activity is detected, users should avoid panic. Emotional reactions often lead to poor decisions. Instead, individuals should approach the situation methodically. The goal is to gather information, assess the situation, and take appropriate action. While urgency is important, careful decision-making is equally critical. Acting too quickly without understanding the nature of the problem can sometimes worsen the situation.

One of the first priorities during a suspected compromise is containment. Containment involves limiting the attacker's ability to continue accessing systems or information. If malware is suspected, disconnecting the device from the internet may prevent further communication with malicious servers. Airplane mode can temporarily disable wireless connections while the situation is evaluated. If unauthorized account access is suspected, changing passwords immediately may prevent attackers from maintaining access.

Password changes should be performed carefully. If a device is infected with malware capable of recording keystrokes, changing passwords directly on the compromised device may expose new credentials to attackers. In such cases, users should utilize a trusted device whenever possible. Prioritizing email accounts during password changes is especially important because email often serves as the recovery mechanism for many other services.

Multifactor authentication can play a valuable role during incident response. If MFA was not previously enabled, activating it may help prevent attackers from reentering accounts using stolen credentials. If MFA was already enabled, users should review authentication settings to ensure no unauthorized devices or methods have been added. Attackers sometimes attempt to register their own authentication devices to maintain persistent access.

Financial account protection becomes a top priority when breaches involve banking information, payment services, or shopping accounts. Users should contact financial institutions immediately if unauthorized transactions occur or if financial credentials may have been exposed. Many banks offer fraud monitoring services, transaction alerts, account freezes, and dispute processes designed to protect customers from financial losses. Prompt reporting often improves recovery outcomes.

Mobile devices frequently serve as gateways to multiple accounts and services. Therefore, incident response should include a comprehensive review of connected accounts. Email, social media, cloud storage, messaging platforms, shopping services, cryptocurrency wallets, and productivity tools may all require attention. Attackers often use compromised accounts as stepping stones to additional targets. A thorough review helps identify related compromises before further damage occurs.

Malware removal is another critical aspect of recovery. In some cases, security software may successfully identify and remove malicious applications. However, advanced infections may require more extensive measures. Factory resets are sometimes necessary to ensure complete removal of malware. Although restoring a device to factory settings can be inconvenient, it may provide the most reliable method of eliminating persistent threats. Users should ensure important data is backed up before performing resets whenever possible.

Data recovery becomes particularly important following ransomware attacks, device loss, or accidental deletion. Regular backups significantly simplify recovery efforts. Cloud backups, encrypted external storage, and synchronized services allow users to restore important information without relying on compromised systems. The effectiveness of a backup strategy often becomes apparent only after a crisis occurs. Individuals who maintain current backups generally recover more quickly and with less stress.

Privacy considerations should also be addressed during incident response. Personal information exposed during breaches may create long-term risks beyond immediate account compromises. Identity theft, fraud, impersonation, and social engineering attacks may occur weeks or months after initial incidents. Users should monitor accounts, review credit reports, and remain alert for unusual activity following significant breaches.

Incident documentation is often overlooked but highly valuable. Recording what happened, when it occurred, what actions were taken, and which accounts were affected can assist with investigations, insurance claims, legal matters, and future prevention efforts. Documentation provides clarity during stressful situations and helps identify patterns that may otherwise be missed.

Communication plays an important role when incidents affect multiple people. If a compromised account may expose contacts, coworkers, clients, friends, or family members to additional risks, informing them promptly can prevent further harm. For example, attackers who gain access to messaging accounts may use trusted relationships to launch additional phishing attacks. Early notification helps others remain cautious and avoid becoming secondary victims.

Professional assistance may be necessary in certain situations. Cybersecurity specialists, digital forensics experts, financial institutions, legal advisors, and law enforcement agencies may provide valuable support depending on the severity of the incident. Seeking help is not a sign of failure. Complex incidents often require expertise beyond what most individuals possess. Knowing when to seek assistance is an important part of responsible incident management.

Learning from incidents is a crucial part of long-term security improvement. Every breach provides an opportunity to identify weaknesses and strengthen defenses. Questions worth considering include: How did the attack occur? What warning signs were missed? Which protections succeeded? Which safeguards failed? What changes can reduce future risk? Reflection transforms incidents into valuable learning experiences.

Developing an incident response plan before a breach occurs can dramatically improve outcomes. A personal incident response plan may include important contact information, recovery procedures, backup locations, account inventories, authentication details, and reporting resources. Preparation reduces confusion and enables faster decision-making during stressful situations.

Cyber resilience extends beyond preventing attacks. Resilience involves preparing for adversity, responding effectively, recovering efficiently, and continuing operations despite challenges. Individuals with strong resilience recognize that security incidents may occur but refuse to let those incidents cause permanent disruption. Preparation, adaptability, and persistence form the foundation of resilience.

Organizations often conduct incident response exercises to prepare employees for real-world events. Individuals can benefit from similar practices by mentally rehearsing potential scenarios. Considering how to respond to lost devices, phishing attacks, account compromises, or malware infections helps users develop confidence and familiarity before emergencies arise.

The most important lesson is that recovery is possible. Many people feel overwhelmed when security incidents occur. However, with proper response procedures, support resources, and preparation, most incidents can be managed successfully. While recovery may require time and effort, informed action significantly improves outcomes.

Cybersecurity is not defined by whether incidents occur but by how effectively individuals respond when they do. Mistakes, vulnerabilities, and unexpected events are part of the digital landscape. What matters most is the ability to recognize problems, take decisive action, learn from experiences, and emerge stronger than before. By understanding incident response principles, users gain confidence in their ability to handle challenges and protect themselves in an increasingly connected world.

Nathan received a notification

Nathan owned a small online consulting business that depended heavily on mobile technology. His smartphone served as his office, communication center, banking platform, scheduling tool, and customer management system. Nearly every aspect of his business flowed through the device. Although he considered himself reasonably security-conscious, he never imagined how quickly a single incident could disrupt his operations.

One Friday afternoon, Nathan received a notification indicating that someone had attempted to log into his email account from another country. The alert caught his attention, but he assumed it was a harmless mistake. After all, he had occasionally received unusual notifications before. Busy preparing for an upcoming client presentation, he dismissed the warning and continued working.

The following morning, the situation escalated dramatically. Several clients contacted Nathan asking about unusual messages they had received from his email address. The messages contained suspicious links and requested urgent payments. Confused and alarmed, Nathan logged into his account and discovered numerous unauthorized emails had been sent overnight.

As he investigated further, he realized the attackers had gained access to his email account and used it to target his contacts. Several account settings had been modified, including forwarding rules designed to secretly copy incoming messages to an unknown address. The attackers were not only impersonating him but also monitoring his communications.

Initially, Nathan felt overwhelmed. His business reputation was at stake, client trust was threatened, and he had no idea how much information might have been exposed. Panic began to set in. However, he remembered advice from a cybersecurity webinar he had attended months earlier: stay calm, assess the situation, and focus on containment.

Using a trusted laptop, Nathan immediately changed his email password and enabled multifactor authentication. He reviewed account settings, removed unauthorized forwarding rules, and signed out all active sessions. Next, he contacted clients to explain the situation and warn them not to interact with suspicious messages. Although the conversations were uncomfortable, transparency helped preserve trust.

The attackers had also attempted to access several other services linked to his email account. Because Nathan acted quickly, most of these attempts failed. Nevertheless, he spent the remainder of the weekend reviewing every important account, updating credentials, and verifying security settings. The process was time-consuming, but it provided peace of mind.

A cybersecurity consultant later helped Nathan investigate the incident. Together, they determined that the attack likely began through a phishing email received several weeks earlier. The message had appeared to come from a trusted software provider and requested account verification. Nathan vaguely remembered clicking a link and entering credentials during a particularly busy workday. What seemed insignificant at the time had provided attackers with access to his account.

Rather than dwelling on the mistake, Nathan focused on learning from the experience. He developed a personal incident response plan that included emergency contacts, account recovery procedures, backup verification steps, and security review checklists. He also implemented stronger monitoring tools that alerted him to unusual account activity.

Several months later, those preparations proved valuable. While traveling, Nathan accidentally left his smartphone in a rideshare vehicle. In the past, such a situation might have caused significant stress. This time, he followed the procedures outlined in his response plan. Using a secondary device, he accessed remote management tools, activated lost mode, and tracked the phone's location. Because encryption and strong authentication were already enabled, he felt confident that sensitive information remained protected.

The phone was eventually recovered, but the incident reinforced the value of preparation. Nathan realized that security incidents rarely occur at convenient times. Effective response depends on decisions made before problems arise. Planning ahead transforms uncertainty into action.

As his confidence grew, Nathan began discussing cybersecurity more openly with colleagues and clients. He discovered that many successful professionals lacked basic response strategies despite relying heavily on digital technology. Several admitted they would not know what to do if an account were compromised or a device were stolen.

Inspired by these conversations, Nathan organized a workshop focused on personal cybersecurity resilience. Participants learned how to recognize warning signs, contain incidents, recover accounts, and strengthen defenses. Many attendees expressed relief after realizing that cybersecurity incidents, while stressful, were manageable with proper preparation.

One participant, Maria, later contacted Nathan to share her own experience. A phishing attack had compromised one of her accounts, but because she followed the response procedures discussed during the workshop, she contained the incident quickly and avoided significant losses. Her success reinforced Nathan's belief that education and preparation make a meaningful difference.

Years later, Nathan looked back on the email breach as a turning point. At the time, it felt like a crisis. In retrospect, it became one of the most valuable learning experiences of his career. The incident taught him that cybersecurity is not about perfection. It is about resilience, preparation, and continuous improvement.

He understood that future threats would continue emerging. New technologies, attack methods, and vulnerabilities would create ongoing challenges. However, he no longer viewed incidents as catastrophic events. Instead, he saw them as manageable situations requiring informed responses and disciplined action.

Nathan's story illustrates an important truth about cybersecurity. Security incidents can happen to anyone. Intelligence, experience, and caution reduce risk, but they do not eliminate it entirely. What separates successful outcomes from devastating consequences is often the quality of the response.

The lessons Nathan learned apply to individuals, families, and organizations alike. Recognizing problems quickly, containing threats effectively, recovering systematically, and learning from experiences are essential skills in today's digital world. These capabilities transform users from passive victims into active participants in their own protection.

Most importantly, Nathan discovered that confidence comes from preparation. Knowing how to respond reduces fear and uncertainty. Users who develop response plans, maintain backups, understand recovery procedures, and practice good security habits position themselves to overcome challenges successfully.

As mobile technology becomes increasingly central to modern life, incident response and recovery skills will remain critical components of personal cybersecurity. The goal is not to avoid every problem but to build the resilience necessary to navigate difficulties effectively. With preparation, awareness, and determination, individuals can recover from setbacks, strengthen their defenses, and continue moving forward with confidence in an ever-evolving digital world.

The lessons Nathan learned apply to individuals, families, and organizations alike. Recognizing problems quickly, containing threats effectively, recovering systematically, and learning from experiences are essential skills in today's digital world. These capabilities transform users from passive victims into active participants in their own protection.

Most importantly, Nathan discovered that confidence comes from preparation. Knowing how to respond reduces fear and uncertainty. Users who develop response plans, maintain backups, understand recovery procedures, and practice good security habits position themselves to overcome challenges successfully.

As mobile technology becomes increasingly central to modern life, incident response and recovery skills will remain critical components of personal cybersecurity. The goal is not to avoid every problem but to build the resilience necessary to navigate difficulties effectively. With preparation, awareness, and determination, individuals can recover from setbacks, strengthen their defenses, and continue moving forward with confidence in an ever-evolving digital world.

Chapter 9

Building Lifelong Mobile Security Habits and Digital Resilience

One of the greatest misconceptions about cybersecurity is the belief that security is achieved through a single action. Many people assume that installing antivirus software, enabling a password, or updating a device once is enough to remain protected indefinitely. In reality, cybersecurity is not a one-time event. It is an ongoing process that requires consistent habits, awareness, and adaptation. The most secure individuals are not necessarily the most technically skilled. Instead, they are the people who develop strong security habits and apply them consistently over time.

Mobile devices have become deeply integrated into everyday life. Smartphones accompany people from the moment they wake up until they go to sleep. These devices manage communications, finances, healthcare information, business activities, entertainment, transportation, shopping, education, and social relationships. Because smartphones occupy such a central role in modern life, maintaining security requires more than occasional attention. It requires developing habits that become part of everyday behavior.

Habits are powerful because they reduce the need for constant decision-making. When security practices become routine, users are less likely to forget important tasks or make careless mistakes. Just as brushing teeth becomes an automatic part of personal hygiene, cybersecurity habits can become a natural part of digital life. The goal is to make security a lifestyle rather than an occasional reaction to threats.

One of the most important lifelong habits involves maintaining awareness. Cybercriminals frequently rely on distraction, urgency, and emotional manipulation. Individuals who pause before acting, evaluate situations carefully, and remain alert to warning signs are less likely to become victims. Awareness does not require paranoia. Instead, it involves paying attention to unexpected requests, unusual behavior, and situations that seem inconsistent with normal patterns.

Critical thinking is closely connected to awareness. Mobile users encounter enormous amounts of information every day. Emails, text messages, social media posts, advertisements, notifications, and news articles constantly compete for attention. Attackers often disguise malicious content within this flow of information. Developing the habit of questioning unexpected requests and verifying information independently helps prevent many forms of cybercrime.

Password management remains a foundational security habit. Strong, unique passwords significantly reduce the likelihood of unauthorized access. However, maintaining good password practices requires consistency. Users should avoid password reuse, update compromised credentials promptly, and utilize password managers whenever possible. These practices become more effective when applied across all important accounts rather than only a select few.

Multifactor authentication should become a permanent component of digital life. As attackers continue improving credential theft techniques, passwords alone provide insufficient protection for many accounts. MFA creates additional barriers that make unauthorized access significantly more difficult. Users who consistently enable MFA on important services build stronger defenses against a wide range of attacks.

Regular software updates represent another essential habit. Operating systems, applications, browsers, and security tools all require updates to address vulnerabilities and improve protections. Delaying updates often provides attackers with opportunities to exploit known weaknesses. Users who make updates a routine part of device maintenance reduce exposure to many common threats.

Permission reviews should also become a recurring activity. Mobile applications frequently evolve over time, adding features and requesting additional access to device resources. Applications installed months or years earlier may possess permissions that are no longer necessary. Reviewing permissions periodically helps users maintain control over personal information and identify potential privacy concerns before they become serious problems.

Digital organization contributes significantly to security. Many users accumulate large numbers of applications, accounts, subscriptions, and stored files over time. Unused accounts, forgotten applications, and outdated information can create unnecessary risks. Periodically reviewing digital assets allows users to remove unnecessary exposure and simplify security management. A well-organized digital environment is generally easier to secure than a cluttered one.

Data backup habits provide protection against both cyberattacks and accidental losses. Backups are often overlooked until they are needed. Unfortunately, creating backups after a ransomware attack, hardware failure, or device theft is impossible. Effective backup strategies require consistency. Automated cloud backups, encrypted local storage, and periodic verification of backup integrity help ensure information remains recoverable when unexpected events occur.

Privacy management is another area where habits matter. Information shared today may remain accessible for years. Users should regularly review privacy settings, social media visibility controls, advertising preferences, and account permissions. Maintaining awareness of what information is being shared and with whom helps reduce long-term exposure to privacy risks.

Financial security practices deserve special attention. Smartphones increasingly serve as financial management tools, making them attractive targets for cybercriminals. Monitoring account activity, enabling transaction alerts, reviewing statements, and responding quickly to suspicious activity help reduce financial risks. Consistent monitoring often allows users to identify problems before significant losses occur.

Education and continuous learning are critical components of lifelong security. Technology evolves rapidly, and attackers continuously develop new techniques. Security practices that were effective years ago may no longer provide sufficient protection today. Staying informed about emerging threats, security updates, and best practices allows users to adapt proactively rather than reacting after incidents occur.

Digital resilience extends beyond technical protections. Resilience involves the ability to respond effectively to challenges, recover from setbacks, and continue operating despite difficulties. Security incidents can be stressful and disruptive, but resilient individuals approach problems systematically. They understand that recovery is possible and focus on solutions rather than panic. Building resilience requires preparation, confidence, and realistic expectations.

Families play an important role in cybersecurity. Security habits often spread through social influence and shared experiences. Parents can teach children safe technology practices. Spouses can help each other identify suspicious activity. Friends and coworkers can share information about emerging threats. Security becomes stronger when approached as a community effort rather than an isolated responsibility.

Children and teenagers require particular attention because they often adopt new technologies quickly. Teaching younger users about privacy, phishing, social engineering, safe downloading practices, and responsible online behavior helps establish healthy habits early in life. These lessons provide benefits that extend far beyond individual devices and continue into adulthood.

Trust management is another valuable skill. Modern technology depends heavily on trust. Users trust applications, service providers, websites, cloud platforms, financial institutions, and communication systems. However, trust should not be granted blindly. Evaluating trustworthiness, verifying identities, and maintaining healthy skepticism help users navigate digital environments more safely.

One challenge many individuals face is balancing convenience and security. Security measures sometimes introduce additional steps or minor inconveniences. Multifactor authentication requires extra verification. Password managers require setup and maintenance. Software updates may interrupt workflows. The temptation to prioritize convenience is understandable, but small investments in security often prevent much larger disruptions later.

Consistency is perhaps the most important factor in long-term cybersecurity success. Occasional bursts of security activity provide limited protection if followed by long periods of neglect. Modest efforts applied consistently tend to produce better outcomes than intensive efforts applied sporadically. Security is strengthened through repetition and routine.

The concept of digital citizenship emphasizes responsible participation in the online world. Good digital citizens respect privacy, verify information, protect personal data, and contribute to safer digital environments. By adopting responsible habits, individuals not only protect themselves but also reduce risks for others. Cybersecurity benefits communities as much as individuals.

Future technologies will undoubtedly introduce new opportunities and challenges. Artificial intelligence, wearable devices, smart homes, connected vehicles, augmented reality systems, and emerging communication platforms will expand the digital ecosystem. While specific threats will change, strong habits remain effective because they focus on principles rather than technologies. Awareness, verification, preparation, and responsible decision-making continue providing value regardless of how technology evolves.

Ultimately, lifelong mobile security is not about achieving perfection. Mistakes happen. Vulnerabilities emerge. Unexpected events occur. The goal is not to eliminate all risk but to manage risk effectively and respond constructively when challenges arise. Individuals who develop strong security habits create a foundation that supports long-term resilience and confidence.

As this book approaches its conclusion, it is important to recognize that cybersecurity is a journey rather than a destination. The habits, principles, and strategies discussed throughout these chapters provide tools for navigating an increasingly connected world. By applying these lessons consistently, users can strengthen their defenses, protect their information, and enjoy the benefits of technology with greater confidence and peace of mind.

Olivia implemented a password manager

Olivia had always embraced technology. As a marketing consultant, she relied heavily on mobile devices for communication, project management, financial transactions, and client relationships. Her smartphone was never far from reach. Over the years, she downloaded countless applications, created hundreds of accounts, and connected to numerous online services. Like many people, she enjoyed the convenience technology provided but rarely considered the habits that influenced her security.

Everything changed after a minor cybersecurity incident involving one of her social media accounts. Although the compromise caused little damage, the experience exposed weaknesses in her digital practices. She realized that security was not something she actively managed. Instead, she reacted to problems only after they occurred. Determined to improve, Olivia decided to approach cybersecurity differently.

Rather than searching for a single solution, she focused on developing habits. Her first step was organizing her digital life. She reviewed old accounts, removed unused applications, and updated outdated credentials. The process took several weekends, but it revealed how much unnecessary exposure had accumulated over the years. Simplifying her digital environment made it easier to understand and manage.

Next, Olivia implemented a password manager. Initially, the transition felt inconvenient because she had to replace dozens of reused passwords. However, once the system was in place, managing credentials became easier than ever. Each account received a unique password, and she no longer worried about remembering complex combinations. What began as a security measure quickly became a productivity improvement.

Multifactor authentication followed shortly afterward. Olivia enabled MFA on email accounts, banking platforms, cloud storage services, and social media profiles. The extra verification step occasionally required additional effort, but she appreciated the added protection. Knowing that stolen passwords alone could not compromise her accounts provided reassurance.

Over time, these practices became routine. Security was no longer something she thought about only when problems occurred. It became part of her daily workflow. Software updates were installed promptly. Permissions were reviewed regularly. Backups occurred automatically. Suspicious messages were verified before action was taken. Small habits gradually formed a comprehensive security strategy.

Several years later, Olivia encountered a situation that demonstrated the value of her efforts. A major data breach exposed information associated with a popular online service she used. Millions of users were affected, and attackers quickly began attempting credential stuffing attacks against other platforms. Because Olivia used unique passwords for every account, the breach had minimal impact on her. While many users scrambled to secure multiple services, she only needed to update a single credential.

The incident reinforced an important lesson: strong habits often prevent problems before they become visible. Security success is frequently measured by incidents that never occur. Because effective protections operate quietly in the background, users may not realize how many threats have been avoided.

Inspired by her progress, Olivia began sharing cybersecurity tips with friends and family. Her younger brother frequently downloaded applications from unknown sources. Her parents struggled to recognize phishing attempts. Rather than overwhelming them with technical details, Olivia focused on simple habits. Verify unexpected requests. Use unique passwords. Enable multifactor authentication. Review permissions. Maintain backups. These recommendations were practical and easy to understand.

One day, her father received a message claiming that his bank account had been compromised. The message contained a link and requested immediate action. Remembering previous conversations, he avoided the link and contacted the bank directly. The message was fraudulent. A simple habit of verification prevented a potentially costly mistake.

As the years passed, technology continued evolving. Artificial intelligence became more common. Smart home devices multiplied. Digital payment systems expanded. New applications and services appeared constantly. Despite these changes, Olivia noticed that the core principles of security remained remarkably stable. Awareness, preparation, verification, and consistency continued providing protection regardless of technological advances.

Eventually, Olivia began mentoring young professionals entering the workforce. Many were highly skilled with technology but lacked cybersecurity awareness. She often compared security habits to physical health habits. Just as exercise, nutrition, and sleep contribute to long-term well-being, security practices contribute to long-term digital resilience. Small actions performed consistently create meaningful results over time.

One of her mentees, Jacob, experienced a phishing attempt during his first year at a new company. Attackers impersonated a senior executive and requested confidential information. Because Jacob had adopted the verification habits Olivia emphasized, he confirmed the request through another channel before responding. The attack failed. The lesson reinforced his confidence and demonstrated the value of good habits.

Years later, Olivia reflected on her cybersecurity journey. What began as a reaction to a minor incident had evolved into a lifelong commitment to digital responsibility. She realized that the most important change was not technological but behavioral. Her habits shaped her outcomes far more than any individual tool or application.

She understood that cybersecurity was not about fear or suspicion. It was about awareness and responsibility. Technology offered tremendous opportunities for communication, creativity, learning, and growth. Security practices simply ensured those opportunities could be enjoyed more safely and sustainably.

Olivia's story illustrates the power of habits. Major security improvements often result from small, repeated actions rather than dramatic interventions. Strong passwords, timely updates, careful verification, regular backups, and thoughtful permission management may seem simple individually. Together, they create a powerful defense system that grows stronger over time.

The story also demonstrates the importance of resilience. Security incidents may still occur despite best efforts. What matters is the ability to respond, recover, learn, and continue moving forward. Resilient individuals recognize that challenges are part of the digital landscape and prepare accordingly.

As technology continues shaping the future, the habits Olivia developed remain relevant. Devices will change. Applications will evolve. Threats will adapt. Yet the principles of awareness, preparation, responsibility, and continuous learning will continue serving as reliable guides. Users who embrace these principles position themselves for long-term success in an increasingly connected world.

The lessons from Olivia's journey bring together many of the themes explored throughout this book. Mobile security is not a destination reached once and forgotten. It is a lifelong practice built through consistent habits, informed decisions, and a commitment to continuous improvement. By developing these habits, individuals can strengthen their defenses, protect their privacy, and navigate the digital world with confidence for years to come.

continue serving as reliable guides. Users who embrace these principles position themselves for long-term success in an increasingly connected world.

The lessons from Olivia's journey bring together many of the themes explored throughout this book. Mobile security is not a destination reached once and forgotten. It is [illegible] built through consistent habits, informed decisions, and a commitment to continuous improvement. By developing these habits, individuals strengthen their defenses, protect their privacy and navigate the digital world with confidence for years to come.

Final Thoughts: Staying One Step Ahead in the World of Mobile App Security

The journey through this book has revealed an important truth about modern technology: mobile devices have become extensions of our personal, professional, and financial lives. Smartphones are no longer simple communication tools. They serve as digital wallets, business offices, health monitors, entertainment centers, navigation systems, identity managers, and gateways to countless online services. As their importance continues to grow, so does the responsibility to protect them.

One of the most valuable lessons from this book is that cybersecurity is not reserved for experts. Many people assume that security is the responsibility of software developers, technology companies, or cybersecurity professionals. While those groups certainly play important roles, every smartphone user shares responsibility for protecting their information. The decisions individuals make every day—what apps they install, which permissions they approve, how they manage passwords, and how they respond to suspicious messages—have a direct impact on their security.

Throughout this book, we explored how cybercriminals target mobile applications, exploit vulnerabilities, distribute malware, launch phishing attacks, manipulate users through social engineering, and collect valuable personal information. While these threats may seem intimidating, knowledge transforms uncertainty into confidence. Understanding how attacks work removes much of their power. Attackers often succeed because victims do not recognize the warning signs. Awareness changes that equation.

Another key lesson is that technology itself is neither good nor bad. The same tools that create convenience and opportunity can also create risk when used irresponsibly. Mobile applications allow us to connect with others, manage finances, access education, run businesses, and improve our lives in countless ways. The goal is not to fear technology but to use it wisely. Security enables people to enjoy the benefits of innovation while minimizing unnecessary exposure to threats.

Cybersecurity is best understood as risk management rather than risk elimination. No device, application, or security product can guarantee complete protection against every possible threat. New vulnerabilities will emerge. Attackers will continue adapting. Technologies will evolve. The objective is not perfection. The objective is resilience. Resilient users understand risks, implement safeguards, prepare for incidents, and recover effectively when challenges arise.

One of the strongest themes throughout this book has been the importance of habits. Security is rarely determined by a single decision. Instead, it results from small actions repeated consistently over time. Installing updates promptly, reviewing permissions regularly, using unique passwords, enabling multifactor authentication, verifying unexpected requests, and maintaining backups may seem simple individually. Collectively, these habits create powerful layers of defense that significantly reduce risk.

The concept of defense in depth remains one of the most valuable strategies in cybersecurity. Relying on a single security measure creates vulnerability. Layered protections provide resilience. Strong passwords work alongside multifactor authentication. Security awareness complements technical safeguards. Backups support recovery efforts. Privacy settings reduce data exposure. Each layer contributes to a stronger overall security posture.

Privacy and security are closely connected. Information has become one of the most valuable resources in the modern world. Companies collect data for business purposes, while cybercriminals seek information for fraud, identity theft, surveillance, and financial gain. Understanding how information is collected, stored, shared, and protected empowers individuals to make informed choices about their digital lives. Protecting privacy is not about hiding; it is about maintaining control.

As technology continues evolving, mobile devices will become even more integrated into everyday activities. Artificial intelligence, wearable technology, smart homes, digital payments, connected vehicles, and emerging communication systems will expand the role smartphones play in society. These innovations will create exciting opportunities while introducing new security considerations. Users who develop strong foundational habits today will be better prepared for the technologies of tomorrow.

Artificial intelligence deserves special attention because it will shape the future of both cybersecurity and cybercrime. AI-powered tools can improve threat detection, automate security analysis, and strengthen defenses. At the same time, attackers will use AI to create more convincing phishing campaigns, generate realistic deepfakes, automate reconnaissance activities, and personalize scams. The future will require even greater emphasis on verification, critical thinking, and awareness.

The human element will remain central to cybersecurity regardless of technological advances. Many attacks succeed not because systems fail but because people are manipulated into making decisions that benefit attackers. Social engineering exploits trust, urgency, fear, curiosity, and emotion. Technology can help identify threats, but informed judgment remains one of the most powerful security tools available. Individuals who think critically and verify information independently are far less likely to become victims.

Families also play an important role in cybersecurity. Security habits are often learned through observation and shared experiences. Parents can teach children responsible digital behavior. Friends can warn each other about scams. Coworkers can share information about emerging threats. Building a culture of security strengthens protection for entire communities. Cybersecurity is most effective when knowledge is shared rather than isolated.

Resilience is another critical concept. Security incidents may occur despite best efforts. Devices may be lost. Accounts may be compromised. Malware infections may happen. What matters most is the ability to respond effectively. Preparation transforms crises into manageable situations. Users who maintain backups, understand recovery procedures, and develop incident response plans recover more quickly and with less disruption than those who approach security reactively.

One encouraging reality is that most cybercriminals are opportunists. They often target individuals who present the easiest opportunities rather than the most valuable targets. Basic security measures eliminate many of the vulnerabilities attackers commonly exploit. Strong passwords, multifactor authentication, software updates, cautious app installation practices, and awareness of phishing attacks provide substantial protection against a large percentage of threats encountered by everyday users.

Continuous learning is essential because cybersecurity never stands still. New attack methods, technologies, and risks emerge regularly. Staying informed does not require becoming a cybersecurity expert. Even modest efforts to understand current trends and best practices can significantly improve outcomes. Curiosity, adaptability, and a willingness to learn are valuable assets in an ever-changing digital landscape.

As you complete this book, remember that cybersecurity is a journey rather than a destination. There will never be a moment when security is permanently finished. Instead, it is an ongoing process of awareness, improvement, and adaptation. Every update installed, every suspicious message verified, every password strengthened, and every permission reviewed contributes to a safer digital experience.

The knowledge you have gained throughout these chapters provides a foundation for protecting yourself, your family, your finances, your business, and your digital identity. The threats discussed in this book are real, but they are not unbeatable. Informed users possess powerful advantages. Awareness, preparation, and responsible habits dramatically reduce risk and improve resilience.

Most importantly, remember that technology should serve you—not control you. Mobile devices are tools designed to improve life, enhance productivity, foster communication, and create opportunity. Security allows you to use these tools with confidence. By applying the principles discussed throughout this book, you can enjoy the benefits of modern technology while protecting what matters most.

The digital world will continue changing. New applications will emerge. New services will appear. New threats will develop. Yet the principles of awareness, verification, privacy, responsibility, and resilience will remain timeless. Carry these lessons forward, continue learning, and remain proactive in protecting your digital life. The investment you make in cybersecurity today will continue paying dividends for years to come.

The knowledge you have gained throughout these chapters provides a foundation for protecting yourself, your family, your finances, your business, and your digital identity. The threats discussed in this book are real, but they are not unbeatable. Informed users possess powerful advantages. Awareness, preparation, and responsible habits dramatically reduce risk and improve resilience.

Most importantly, remember that technology should serve you—not control you. Mobile devices are tools designed to improve life, enhance productivity, foster communication, and create opportunity. Security allows you to use these tools with confidence. By applying the principles discussed throughout this book, you can enjoy the benefits of modern technology while protecting what matters most.

The digital world will continue evolving. New applications will emerge. New devices will appear. New threats will develop. Yet the principles of awareness, verification, privacy, responsibility, and resilience will remain timeless. Carry these lessons forward, continue learning, and remain proactive in protecting your digital life. The investment you make in cybersecurity today will continue paying dividends for years to come.

www.ingramcontent.com/pod-product-compliance
Lightning Source LLC
LaVergne TN
LVHW030726061126
851857LV00019B/2013